MW00770212

THE COCKER MAN

THE COCKER MAN

Hedley Millington

Edited by
Tim Jennings

A Nancarrow Publication

Published in 2004 by
Nancarrow Publications
Hollybush Farm
Bissoe
Truro
Cornwall TR4 8TF

ISBN: 0-9547298-0-3

Designed and produced by The Studio Publishing Services Ltd, Exeter EX4 8JN

Printed in Great Britain

The Cocker Man is dedicated to all my
'little people', the cocker spaniels who have
played such an important part in my life,
and to Jo Rickards, a true friend.

CONTENTS

Forewords

I felt very honoured when Hedley asked me to write a foreword to his book. We came to the acquaintance of the cocker spaniel very late, but luckily not too late.

After my husband's first stroke, Nicky Phillip's little black cocker bitch that Robin had always loved and admired had a litter of puppies.

Nicky felt that it would be really good for Robin to have the responsibility of caring for and training a puppy, to help get him back together, so he invited him to come and choose which puppy he wanted. We all went, Robin and our three sons. We watched him carefully as he made his selection. He chose the shyest of them all. She has grown into the most wonderful bitch called Slipper and because of her we met Hedley.

Robin and I were in London having dinner with friends when Mark Birley arrived extremely late. He said to me how awful it was he was so late but he had been detained by the most beautiful female. Somehow I felt it must be a bitch. I asked him and he said it was. He then told me all about Hedley and his fantastic spaniels and I said I had to go to Cornwall to see him. He also told me that whenever he went away he would only ever leave his dogs with Hedley. Quite a drive from London to Truro!

I went because I wanted to see for myself and we also wanted to breed from Slipper.

Everything Mark had told me was true. It was wonderful. The dogs that I met were happy, full of enthusiasm and humour. It was an amazing experience.

Slipper went twice because she did not get pregnant the first time. She then had three wonderful puppies, our 'grand-dogs', Snap who is ours and Ben and Indy who belong to our son Robin and his wife Stephanie. They are three really amazing dogs and now we are trying for great grandchildren. Both Snap and Indy went to Hedley earlier last year but sadly did not get in pup. But we will try again. Hopefully, by the time you read this, Hedley will have had more effect on our lives!

I will always be deeply grateful to Mark Birley. Without him we may never have met Hedley and that would be a great loss. He is someone who really understands what the important things in life are and when you sit and have a cup of tea with him, you feel how silly you are to get involved in so many things of no importance.

Thank you Hedley for our wonderful dogs and for being who you are.

Henrietta, Dowager Duchess of Bedford

What can I say about Hedley? He is the original dog whisperer – and on my behalf he has whispered wonderfully to Bella, an Alsatian, and to Jennifer, a black Labrador. Hedley has an eye for and a perception of dogs that is unique in my experience.

One day at his home in Cornwall I was in his kitchen with seven cocker spaniels. We wandered out into the garden – none of the dogs followed but he called each one by name and each one came out to him, one after the other. Miraculous!

He is like a large oak tree under which dogs grow up and thrive under this benevolent umbrella.

Originally we met through my beloved friend Jo Rickards, who herself was extraordinarily perceptive about dogs, and people.

Hedley belongs to a vanishing breed of sturdy, no-nonsense countrymen.

Mark Birley

List of illustrations

Section I

Section II

Section III

Section IV

Introduction

Born in 1932 at Woodlands near Doncaster, Hedley Millington spent much of his childhood with his mother's father, a gamekeeper. At the same time Hedley's parents were harbouring thoughts that he might become an accountant when he grew up. Accountancy's loss has been the countryside's gain.

Hedley bought his first Cocker, a little show bred bitch called Bramble, some 24 years ago. He never saw her mother, who'd supposedly had a caesarean and was unwell.

Hedley worked Bramble in the line on the shoot he keepered. She yelped a bit and was a poor retriever, but he still liked her.

Then when Bramble was five years old she went blind and Hedley realised that her mother had been blind, too, and that he had been conned by an unscrupulous breeder who was whelping from a bitch with progressive retinal atrophy.

It was a disturbing, one might think an off-putting, introduction to the breed, but not for a man of Hedley Millington's mettle.

In fact, he learnt two things from that experience.

The first was an affection for the breed that led him to seek out a working-bred dog and embark on an extraordinary relationship with Cockers.

The second was a determination to never knowingly mislead a client. That has led to an unsurpassed reputation for honesty in a man who has bred one of the dominant strains in the modern, resurgent, working Cocker.

Now he has decided to tell his story and to pass on some of the secrets of his success in trialling and training.

The Cocker Man, though, is not just another training manual, as it contains his philosophy, anecdotes and observations, with nuggets of great advice woven into the fabric of the story.

He will tell of his astonishing scrape with death in front of Her Majesty the Queen, of his admiration for Prince Charles, of his own battle with cancer spanning two decades, and of the healing power of man's best friend.

Hedley talks, controversially and candidly, about the brutal men of the gun dog world who beat their dogs into obedience, then wonder why their dogs are inhibited in the shooting field.

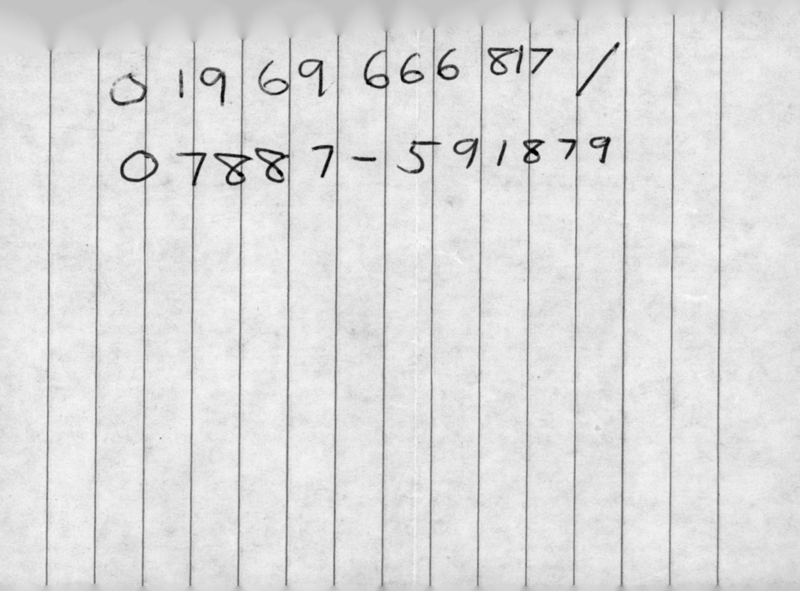

01969 666817 /
07887-591879

Camaro

With the Cocker now regaining popularity and becoming a welcome sight on more and more shoots, he talks, again controversially, about the breeders who have tried to take short cuts to Field Trial success by introducing Springer blood into the breed. Hedley derides these Sprocker breeders and tells how he believes the way forward for the Cocker is through steadily improving the true stock.

His tips and advice, drawn from years of experience, relate to the Cocker, not the Springer, as he will not follow the path of those in innumerable articles, manuals and training videos that conveniently lump the 'Pocket Rocket' in with the Springer.

Cockers, he asserts, are a different Spaniel requiring different expectations, a different approach and a different mind-set in order to get to grips with them. As many will know, Hedley is a panel judge for the Kennel Club, and has judged the French three-day international Cocker championships, as well as Cocker events in Texas.

Hedley Millington's story will fascinate any gun dog enthusiast. It will certainly be the talk of the Spaniel world, because of the controversial nettles grasped for the first time in any gun dog book.

CHAPTER ONE

'Just watch this'

These days on a summer's evening the thing I most enjoy is slipping away to visit my special place – fourteen acres of hidden beauty in a fold of the Cornish countryside.

There was already a large pond tucked in the middle when I bought the land a few years ago. With the help of an excavator I soon re-established a series of ponds, fringed with willow herb and meadow-sweet, all fed by clear spring water.

Then I sat back and let nature do the rest, until now I can rest my eyes and enjoy the result.

In summer big carp rise like hungry piglets and suck at the bread that I throw on the water's mirrored surface, swans glide nearby and warblers busy themselves with their secret life in the reeds.

Winter brings a good fall of woodcock and the ponds are a haven for parcels of duck that see out winter in the shelter of its native oak, ash and alder.

As one who has walked and worked in nature's setting all my life, as a gamekeeper and professional trainer, I am, perhaps, more reflective than when I was a younger man.

Like many a shooting man I'm as happy enjoying the sight of nature's bounty as taking from it.

Even so, you'll never find me here or in many other places without a brace or more of working cockers at my feet.

To see the little dogs bustling and questing in cover is an undiminished joy. Energetic, mercurial and brave, nosy in the very real sense of the word, they are, to my mind, at once merry and earnest in their work.

I believe the raw pleasure of working a good spaniel, though, is just part of what they give us. As I reflect on what cockers have given me – set against what I have given them – I realise that I have had by far the best of the deal.

Over the years I have had deeply satisfying victories in field trials, unforgettable days in the shooting field, both formal and pottering, yet they are burned in my memory because of the work put in by my dogs. But there has been much, much more. Cockers have been my passport to friendships with people from all sections of society, from members of the Royal family and the aristocracy, to princes who were poor men, too, and honest country folk whose experiences were and are pure gold. All have one thing in common, the genuine love of an honest working dog.

I have also witnessed personal tragedies and had my own battles with illness during which I have learnt the spiritual strength that can be gleaned from partnership with a working dog.

Then there's the humour. I swear you couldn't put a price on the laughter and enjoyment I have had down the years with my chosen breed.

I hope to convey some of that fun to you in the following pages, together with the experiences and many insights that a spaniel man might find useful, interesting and downright controversial.

In order to do this I must first introduce the hero and occasional villain of the piece, the working bred cocker spaniel.

I think the best way to describe the character and ability of a cocker is to give you some examples that neatly sum up the quixotic nature of these angelic rascals.

Some of my favourite days in the past were pottering forays with Lord Falmouth and trusty Sooty and Sweep, my first proper cockers.

His lordship and I would wander the hedges and the ponds in the afternoon and he would perhaps shoot five or six pheasants. It was relaxing, we enjoyed the dog work and then in the evening I would go off to feed my pheasants while Lord Falmouth would go to the big house.

There was a flighting pond about a mile from where I lived and I would meet his lordship later out at the pool where he would flight some duck. Sometimes I was not on time to meet him if something had cropped up with the birds or if there was some small problem that needed attention.

At any rate, I would wander out there in the falling light of dimpsey but if I were indeed late I would usually hear two or three shots from the flight path. His lordship was out there and on the ducks. But, as I walked out there, I was invariably alone, no Sooty, no Sweep. And when I arrived at the pond there I would find them, one each side of his lordship, with a couple of duck or more already laid at his side.

'Oh, they arrived a quarter of an hour ago,' he would say as if it were the most natural thing in the world to keep a shooting appointment with two dogs. They, of course, had been bang on time and had no intention of missing the action because their master was tardy.

I, on the other hand, was made to feel thoroughly surplus to requirements, which, truth to tell, was exactly the case. That is the brainpower and character of the little cocker.

My little bitch Ronda was a cocker from top to toe and a cheerful character who was fabulous company. Her Kennel Club name was Loch Cara Brownie, and she was chocolate brown, small, even for a cocker, but she was a field trial champion (F.T.Ch.).

We were running in a trial and during her run in a very small spinney she flushed a very large brown hare which ran out of the spinney to my right and ran down the hedge further away.

With that, the gun by my side fired twice at the hare, but the hare continued. 'Damnit, I missed it.'

'Thank goodness for that,' I thought, because this hare was literally as big as my Ronda. The hare carried on another hundred yards or more, cut through the spinney and went right across the field on the left-hand side, then dropped.

To this the keeper shouted 'That hare is dead.' It had run on wounded before succumbing and now it was 400 yards away. I thought 'Oh my God.'

Then the order came: 'Send your dog Hedley.' Out she went to the line, took it and followed it right through the spinney across the field to the hare, picked it up and brought it back as proud as punch. Though not as proud as I was. That's the guts and stamina of a cocker. They'll always rise to the challenge.

I was in Scotland a few years ago with my big strong cocker Buster, F.T.Ch. Wernffrwd Bunterson, when Mervyn Hendry, a friend, asked if I had ever shot blackcock. I hadn't and he assured me that he would take me on the moor where I could try my luck on these spectacular birds.

I shot two and that was quite enough. I can now rightly claim to have shot the species. But before we accounted for our blackcock, Buster flushed a covey of about nine grouse. I shot one, but my friend, a better shot, had a left and right, plucking a brace from the covey out of my sight.

Buster picked my grouse, then we went to assist my friend quickly, collecting one of his brace, but try as he might Buster could not find the other.

I knew my friend to be a precise shot and not one to claim a hit he hadn't made, so we persisted and were at it in thick heather for about thirty minutes. Suddenly to my left I saw a grouse dash out of the heather and about four seconds later Buster emerged right on his line.

The bird was picked and when we examined the situation we found that the heather had grown over a gully in the ground, forming a tight tunnel some thirty yards long.

The grouse might have thought he was safe from discovery here, but he reckoned without the quite astonishing abilities of a cocker, notably the power of a cocker's nose.

Few dogs would have found that bird, and larger dogs would have given that tunnel up as a bad job, even if they'd got a touch of the scent. Not a cocker. 'Once scented, never left' seems to be their motto.

But there's another side to cockers, a side that's unpredictable yet loveable. Ronda is a good illustration.

Running her in the North Western Counties open qualifier she ran well under the first judge and was running well under the second. She was about to end her run when she flushed a rabbit which was shot a fair way out when the judge gave the order 'Send your dog.' Halfway out she flushed another rabbit, which was shot too.

The judge wanted the first rabbit, so I handled her beyond the second one with no difficulty. She picked the rabbit and headed back to me, me with my hands in my pockets, a smile on my face. All I had to do now was collect the prize. I had won. All she had to do was return with the rabbit.

All was fine until she passed the second rabbit, spat the first one out and picked up the new one to bring it to me. All thoughts of winning evaporated in a split second.

I had rueful reflections as I drove down the motorway with Ronda sitting alongside me. She of course was completely unruffled by the whole situation. After all, one rabbit is pretty much like another.

Ah well, that's my cocker. Whatever they do, good or bad, they seem to be saying 'Just watch this.'

CHAPTER TWO

Hooked

My first cocker taught me my harshest lesson in the dog world, a lesson that's formulated my outlook on 'dog trading' and has stuck with me ever since.

At the time I was a partridge keeper on Sir George Meyrick's estate at Hinton Admiral in Hampshire. As far as spaniels were concerned I was completely green.

I had always somehow fancied a cocker as a canine partner in my keepering duties and responded when I saw a litter advertised by a local kennels. I was shown a very attractive six-week-old puppy and decided that was the one for me. I was not allowed to see the mother, however, and at this point the alarm bells should have started ringing. I was told she was recovering from a caesarean and I accepted that, although today I know a bitch taking that long to recover would be more likely dead.

The little bitch I bought was show bred and I called her Bramble. As time went on she hunted reasonably well, but she was no sort of retriever. She tended to be a little yappy, one of the faults that can be put down to her show breeding lines.

For all that I loved the little dog and she became a good companion in the covers, though never at a peg.

It was five years on that I discovered the truth when Bramble began to go blind with what the vet diagnosed as the hereditary condition progressive retinal atrophy.

Now I knew why I could not be allowed to see the mother. No doubt she was already blind. I imagine she stumbled around, colliding with walls and living an unhappy existence while her unscrupulous owners used her as a sightless breeding machine.

They were out and out sharks and I cannot to this day think of them without harbouring the illest of thoughts and wishes.

What I learnt is how it feels to be done by cruel double dealers and I resolved that I would never sell anyone a puppy until they had seen the mother and if possible the father.

When I got into breeding I also joined in the scheme run by the British Veterinary Association so that my breeding dams and sires are all tested by a qualified veterinary eye specialist. I believe these vets have to study for an extra three years to qualify in this field.

My nearest specialist – Mr Warren – is 70 miles away in Tavistock, but the time and money for the journey is well spent and the results are entered on the Kennel Club registration. Needless to say that I will not breed from a dog with suspect eyesight.

Bramble lived with us in the house until she was eleven, she never wanted for love or affection and I think fondly of her as my introduction to cockers, albeit a faltering one.

She taught me another lesson, namely that what I didn't need in a dog was yapping and an inability to retrieve. Thanks for that Bramble.

I was back at square one with a blind dog, but still with a love of cockers and a better all round understanding of what was required.

I was now looking for a working bred cocker and I eventually found that stalwart of Welsh field sports, John Carter, the keeper at Coldbrook Park near Abergavenny, who was breeding under the name of Gaudins Gundogs.

John now lives on Exmoor and I see him from time to time at trials; I believe he still runs the occasional cocker.

At any rate I bought my first true working cocker from him. Her official name was Gaudins Psyche, but I called the little black bitch Sooty.

She was a lovely bitch, a good hunter and a nice retriever, although she tended to have a sulky temperament. I decided to get another, so by now you can guess I was hooked. I loved the true cocker action and plucky hunting spirit of the breed.

I went back to John and bought Gaudins Sweep. No prizes for guessing her pet name, so Sooty and Sweep it was in the beating line.

Then out of the blue, while keepering on the Isle of

Wight, I got a call from a policeman in Wales who said he had a two year old blue roan bitch called Morborne Tell for sale. He'd found her too hard to handle, and he knew I was looking for good dogs.

I drove up to Wales and found a small bitch. She was timid and looked as though butter wouldn't melt in her mouth. How many of us have been deceived by the doe eyes of a cocker? I was about to buy a ball of fire.

I had moved now and was head keeper to Lord Falmouth on his Cornish estate at Tregothnan, with Sooty, Sweep and Gina schooling me in the art of dog handling. Boy, was I learning?

Once bonded to me these dogs were going nowhere until they went to the happy hunting ground in the sky. But I was seriously addicted by now, no longer just hooked. I needed more and better stock and nothing was going to stop me.

Fate took a hand with a call from a friend in Hampshire, a springer man who had come by a 14-month-old working cocker bitch. She was very well bred, was I interested?

I saw Trixie at a working test near Aldershot. She was shown to me soaking wet and looking thoroughly miserable. In her pedigree were two names that were the springboard for many fine cockers – Monnow Elizabeth and Monnow Mayfly.

I wasn't interested in this pathetic looking thing, though. 'Thanks, but no thanks.'

Then as I walked away I looked back at Trixie's huddled little figure and something made me say 'Oh for God's sake put her in the car,' nine words I have never regretted.

1 Hedley at David Hoare's Luscombe Castle with F.T. Chs. Swallow Law Snipe and Loch Cara Brownie

2 *Buster, F.T. Ch. Wernffrwd Bunterson*

3 Nancarrow Gypsy

4 Migdale Ben, a real good friend

5 Mervyn Hendry, Hedley and a Scottish keeper enjoy a day out on the moors

6 Hedley and Cyril Gwynne

7 Hedley and Lord Falmouth enjoy a day's shooting with Widgeon and Sooty at Caerhayes Castle

8 *Nancarrow Amoretto (Lass) and Maesydderwyn Kestrel (Scamp)*

9 *Beryl Chappell's painting of Bournepark Blaze of Nancarrow*

10 Nancarrow Harry picking up at Luscombe Castle

I knew she was different when I got her home and put her in a kennel with a six-foot weld-mesh run. I went indoors for a brew of tea and a few minutes later heard a scratching on the woodwork. It was Trixie. I was certain I had fastened the gate to the run, but anyway back she went to the kennel.

This time the latch was properly fastened, but I watched from the kitchen window as Trixie scaled the six-foot fence like a commando and ran to the back door. 'Well old girl, if you want to come in here that badly, so you shall,' I told her.

She'd never been in a house before, but immediately made herself at home. Later I changed her name to Pixie and we spent many happy years together.

Her previous owner had not been able to get her to retrieve and even tried forced retrieving on her, a method I will not entertain. We soon got to understand each other and Pixie became first an enthusiastic and then a brilliant retriever.

Now I had four sound bitches around me and I was looking for a suitable dog. I turned to the Hon. Fiona Hopkinson, she of the Burnhatch prefix name, choosing her black roan dog Burnhatch Brig.

I remember the first time I went to Fiona's place near Reading. We went out to try and get a mating, but Fiona's husband was frightened that Sooty was going to snap, so he tied a piece of bandage around her muzzle.

We tried for two or three hours, but to no avail.

Fiona, who was quite a character, had been busy indoors watching horse racing on television and when she came outside she asked if there had been any success.

'Afraid not,' came the reply.

'Right then', said Fiona, 'can that damn thing of yours hunt, Hedley?'

'Well, I wouldn't be here if he couldn't, Fiona.'

With that she took us off down the fields. The dogs flushed a rabbit or two and a couple of mallard as we walked around the pond. The next thing you know they were mated.

That's how Morborne Tell was mated to 'Brig' and the union produced my first field trial champion Nancarrow Gypsy.

At this time Fiona was selling up to return to Scotland which was a little bit too far for me to travel to stud, so I drove to Reading and bought Brig from her.

Brig was never a trialling dog, but was good in line and produced outstanding pups. He went to Pixie and that mating produced my second champion Nancarrow Sooty.

Gypsy was a small bitch, a superb little thing, nice to handle, a great hunter and superb retriever, but she had a wicked side to her and was not the kind of dog I wanted to produce.

I bought another dog called Migdale Ben from my old friend Harry Hardwicke. Harry had won an open qualifying stake with him, but I think he had lost interest in the dog, so I bought Ben, or Jet as his kennel name was, and discovered that he had the sort of temperament that I liked.

Ask him and he would rule the world for you, tell him and he wouldn't bother. We got on fine. I ran him at the Cocker Club trials in Scotland, won it and made Migdale Ben into a F.T.Ch.

Then I went to visit old friend Jack Wintle of legendary Geordieland Dogs. Jack had a liver roan called Geordieland Rob Roy, and I bought him from Jack and gave him one of the pups from the first litter he sired.

A lot of people benefited from Jack's breeding and his development of the cocker. I was among them. All good things in the world of genuine cockers today trace back to Jack and I am proud that the last cocker he owned was a Nancarrow dog.

With Rob Roy in the kennel, together with my other proven dogs and bitches, I was on the way to producing the nucleus of the sort of cocker I had in mind. When Rob Roy died we planted the species of rose of the same name on his grave.

I heard about a black dog called Heath Hill Lad, a terrific hunting dog with a heavy punch and the drive required for top competition.

I agreed a price for him and went to collect him, but I was told then that he was no longer for sale, but that a dog called Swallowlaw Snipe was available. I bought Snipe, who turned out to be the finest buy of any cocker I ever made.

Snipe and I clicked from the beginning. He was well built, with terrific character and temperament, but he had not been going at the right speed until he and I got together. From then on he was a winner. There's no explaining it – we just clicked.

Good class, quality bitches were brought to be mated with Snipe by colleagues who had seen him perform in trials, but I would not take a fee from those I fancied. I preferred to have the pick of the litter.

In this way I built up a formidable kennel of top quality dogs, and especially top notch breeding bitches.

That's how I got my favourite bitch of all time, Bournepark Blaze of Nancarrow or Pebble, through my old friend Cyril Gwynne from Wales. On her day Pebble was untouchable. There wasn't a dog in the country to match her when she was in the mood.

Pebble was fantastic, but when she didn't want to perform you might as well pack up and go home. Her half sister Kate, Wernffrwd Enfys, was consistent and a fine dog, but lacked the diamond sparkle of Pebble in full flight.

We mated Pebble to Heathill Lad and I had also bought a dog called Wernffrwd Bunterson, which gave me two lines that I could cross out to Snipe puppies.

That became the mainstay of the Nancarrow line. Pebble had four litters and I kept most of the bitches to form the nucleus of what I wanted for my own stock.

Now we had great stock and I could go out confidently and run with the best in the country, because we were up there with the best. We could take on anything anywhere at the time.

I was now set on the path that was to take me up and down the country, meeting some of the finest folk you could ever want to meet, the trialling fraternity.

CHAPTER THREE

Spare the rod, make the cocker

If sitting on your lap makes a dog a lapdog, then that's what mine are. I like nothing better than to have them close to me for a bit of spoiling. After all, the wee dogs run through brambles and bracken to give me my sport, so the odd bit of affection is a small price to pay for not having to get down on all fours and flush a rabbit out of the nettles myself!

I make light of it, but it is a serious business. Discipline is at the heart of the matter. How hard do you treat a spaniel? I say not hard at all, because there is simply no benefit to doing so.

The modern spaniel has been bred to be so biddable for the most part as to make beating it a completely futile act of brutality.

So listen to me very carefully, for listening is at the heart of this.

The secret is in your voice.

From its youngest days when it first ventures outside, scurrying round your feet, encourage and admonish with your voice, not your hand.

If he runs on too far, growl at him. As soon as he turns to come back to you, raise the pitch of your voice, not your hand.

Don't be afraid to shout at him, but fear thrashing him, for it could ruin his trust in you forever.

Always be ready to pursue the miscreant out across the landscape. Grab him by all means, give him a good shaking. Why not? Stare him hard in the eyes and utter murderous thoughts, of course, but beat him, never.

I'll tell you two stories that encapsulate my philosophy, then later some others that do not that I find repugnant.

I was once walking back to my car after a trial when I heard two other handlers making disparaging remarks about another handler's bitch. 'It'll never win anything that one,' said one, 'It's soft, it lives indoors.'

I listened with a smile on my face, because the dog at my heel had just won the trial. She sleeps at the foot of my bed.

On another occasion I was in the rabbit pen with a friend watching him as he ran to stop his cocker dog that had just chased a rabbit.

He grabbed the villain, picked him up and shook him, but when the dog gave a squeak he dropped him to the ground, saying 'Sorry old boy, I didn't mean to hurt you.'

That's the sort of handler I like to call my friend, that's the sort of person I like to train with. And by the way, his dog had its first season's shooting not so long afterwards and it never let him down.

As for beatings, many prefer to call them 'hard handling' as if a soft name can give a soft face to something. I prefer to call a spade a spade and confront cruelty with its own name.

I fully expect to be criticised for what I say here, but I'm prepared for that because I believe the future of our sport depends on us being honest and direct.

I do not believe the hunting of a bird or an animal for the kill is cruel. There is nothing more natural than, for instance, a spaniel questing through cover to put a rabbit in the aim of his human partner.

On the other hand there is nothing natural or sportsmanlike about a man systematically beating that same spaniel to control or direct its behaviour or to punish it when it doesn't behave in the required manner.

I'm ashamed that, over the years, I have witnessed unnecessary and cruel punishments in the field and sometimes, more damningly, at the end of a trial when a handler will take it out on the dog simply because he hasn't been placed.

I have heard countless other stories of the harshness and unfairness of handlers, albeit a few, but still far too many.

I have even heard of one well-known trialler having a spaniel hanging from an onion set in a garage while he beat it. I didn't see this and I couldn't prove it, but my blood boiled just hearing it and I'm sorry to say that I've seen enough myself to give that report credence.

Two ladies I know witnessed another well-known trialler after he'd taken the dog back to his car. Peeved that the dog had let him down, he thoroughly beat him believing he was unobserved.

The dog was so savagely laid upon that it had to be helped into the back of the vehicle before this travesty of a handler could leave.

One of the ladies happened to be an official of the club and duly reported the incident, later raised at the AGM. Quite rightly so. And this man's punishment? A two-year ban, would you believe?

But what happened then? Everyone abhorred the dog's treatment, but when I tried to propose that this matter should be passed on to the Kennel Club for action, so began furious back-pedalling.

'He might employ a barrister and then what do we do?' came the voice of one waverer. The consequence was that the club shunned its responsibility to the creature that gives us our sport and has no voice of its own – the dog.

At another recent trial Kathy my wife was in tears when I returned to the car. Enquiring what was wrong, she told me she had just witnessed pure spite and cruelty.

Once again a thwarted competitor – someone who should have known better – was teaching his dog a lesson for letting him down. The dog had its head banged on the tarmac of a road and was punched on the ribs. Surely that's the work of a coward.

Years ago I ran in a trial that I was lucky enough to win. The keepers generously offered to give us a training session the next day and shoot rabbits over our dogs for us.

We met up and in the line of guns was a shepherd called, appropriately, Big Jock.

No sooner had the dog work begun than several handlers started doling out punishments totally unwarranted for 'crimes' committed by their dogs.

Big Jock turned to them in disbelief. 'You lot of bastards. I took a day off to have a day's pleasure and watch some good dog work, not to watch you knock hell out of your dogs.'

He was not a soft man and doubtless had trained border collies himself, but his words should be noted carefully. If a Highland shepherd found this totally unacceptable, what are our town cousins going to think of it?

On another occasion in Scotland I was staying with a keeper friend who asked if I would go with a young friend of his into the heather to shoot some rabbits because he was having problems with his cocker running in.

This young chap was pleasant company and I was looking forward to an enjoyable morning, but no sooner had we let the dogs out of our cars than he took a piece of plastic hose out of his pocket and proceeded to thrash a dog with it.

'What the hell's going on,' I asked.

'I always let him know what's what before I start,' came his reply.

I was a guest and bit my tongue thinking that would be that, but there were more beatings for the dog to endure until he turned to me and said enquiringly, 'My dog is not hunting as well as yours.'

I suppose my reply sums up my philosophy about gun dogs. 'I wonder how well you would work if you had to keep looking over your shoulder wondering when you were going to have seven bells knocked out of you?'

He said he'd never thought of it that way, so I explained the way that I and many other quite successful trainers control dogs, with minimal punishment and none of that cruelty. I hoped he took this information on board.

I also hope people absorb the message given by Harry Hardwicke, that fine servant of the spaniel world, in his video on spaniel training for beginners.

'These modern dogs are really soft,' says Harry. He's right. It doesn't mean they won't beat up cover and pursue a runner with all their heart. It simply means they need gentle handling and minimum punishment.

Just a change of tone in the voice does the trick nine times out of a ten and if they are really trying it on, a bit of a shaking does the rest.

This 'treat them hard stuff' is all nonsense.

I was a keeper for most of my career and like all keepers I've had to stand my ground with villains and poachers. But as for beating up dogs, I would rather not own one if I had to do that.

A working dog should be your partner and friend, and that's not a relationship built on fear.

By far the majority of handlers are kind-hearted and concerned and use modern training methods that do not require a good hiding as part of the formula.

You might accuse me of playing into the hand of the antis by even raising the matter publicly, but if this minority is tolerated in our ranks, who is the real threat to our sport?

We will say 'ours is a clean sport' and you can be sure that those who hate what we do and everything we stand for will one day expose us as liars with secretly filmed videos and photographs of the hard handlers in our ranks who are the real threat to our sport.

And whom do we blame then? Worse than that, what about the dogs? Who will speak up for them if we don't?

CHAPTER FOUR

Training . . . Go north, young trialler

There are many fine books and video films outlining training programmes for your gun dog, so I'll try not to duplicate the words of other, mostly wiser, men.

I would, however, recommend the late Peter Moxon's writings on the subject, because he was a very fine trainer of gun dogs.

A lot of people have cocked a snook at Peter because he didn't have a huge collection of silverware from trials and championships on his mantelpiece.

What they don't know, though, is that Peter suffered terribly from match nerves and literally went to pieces if he was called up into the line. He learnt this early on in his career and had to live with it, but

I firmly believe he was as good as most of us at training a dog and better than many.

Training in my view is all about bonding and discipline. I've dealt with discipline elsewhere and I have very strong views about those who bend a dog to their will with pain and punishment. I believe they should be consigned to the knacker's yard of the profoundly unintelligent.

Bonding is a different but related thing and is all about mutual respect and, dare I say it, affection.

The first few weeks of your relationship with a dog – whether you get it as a pup or an older dog – can be a make or break. My advice is to take it steady and show all the patience and affection you can.

With a puppy, don't just shut them away in the kennel and spend little time with them as some do. Don't, though, go to the other extreme of having them running around the house causing mayhem and learning the anarchist philosophy.

Puppies also need a space of their own and time to reflect on the new experiences and the knowledge they are collecting.

What you need is a happy medium.

Have the pup with you when you are about, but have an outside kennel so that he knows that is his place and he will spend time there when he is not with you and where he can do no damage.

Take him out in the car with you, play little games with him, bond with him, but whatever you do, be kind but firm. Don't let him do whatever he wants.

If you want him to do something, make him do it, but remember he's just a baby and he can get bored, so don't make him repeat things. Don't get him bored.

You will be feeding your puppy three or four times a day, so use that important time. Make him wait for his food, make him sit. Introduce him to the first gentle commands and also to louder noises, perhaps a feeding bowl dropped deliberately!

These little things will pay dividends later, but all the time you must remain your puppy's best friend and mentor, always remembering that he is not a machine.

The time after his second set of jabs when he is allowed to go out is vital. Take your puppy to the beach or take him to the High Street. Offer him new experiences so that you are all the time building up his confidence.

By this stage I usually have my puppies retrieving well. One of my secrets is to go to a car boot sale and buy soft, cuddly toys of various shapes and sizes.

By now I am taking a pup into areas where there has been game, but I make absolutely sure I clear the game away. I just want him to get that interesting scent and wonder what it is all about, motivating his interest.

You can now start to get your puppy to 'hup' (to sit or stay) in the usual way, with a squeeze on the bottom. I also introduce a stamp of my foot and eventually I'll get him to sit, just with the stamp of my foot.

With an older dog I give him time to get to know me and, importantly, to get to know my voice. How can I expect a part trained dog to immediately obey me if he's not tuned his ear into my voice and simply doesn't understand me?

Take your time and don't expect miracles, and you may even get a few. I believe that's sound advice and if you take it in conjunction with an even-handed policy of non-violence, I believe it will pay off for you.

And now I'll turn to one of the great joys of training dogs once you've got the basics instilled in your dog.

Many professional spaniel breeders and triallers take the high road for Scotland and spend a week or two giving young hopeful dogs their final polish or fine tuning old hands with an award or two already in the bag.

There's no reason why the non-professional shouldn't head north too. For a gun dog man, especially a spaniel man, it's the dream holiday. Lots of rabbits, lots of cover, your dog in his element and all the game in the world to steady him.

The very practical reason for heading north is quite simply game supply. Even now when there are comparatively plenty of rabbits about in the rest of the country, it still does not compare with the sheer abundance in Scotland.

Like any countryman I love that country with its wide-open spaces and friendly folk with the pace and manners of bygone years.

On the practical side you have a rabbit trialling season during the summer in Scotland, with a chance to test your dogs against superb local opposition and the dogs that colleagues from the South have brought up with them.

That's an invaluable bonus, but the real purpose is to get your dogs among the heather.

11 HRH The Prince of Wales at Arrallas in Cornwall where Hedley did the picking up

12 'Hold it steady please'

13 Exploring puppies

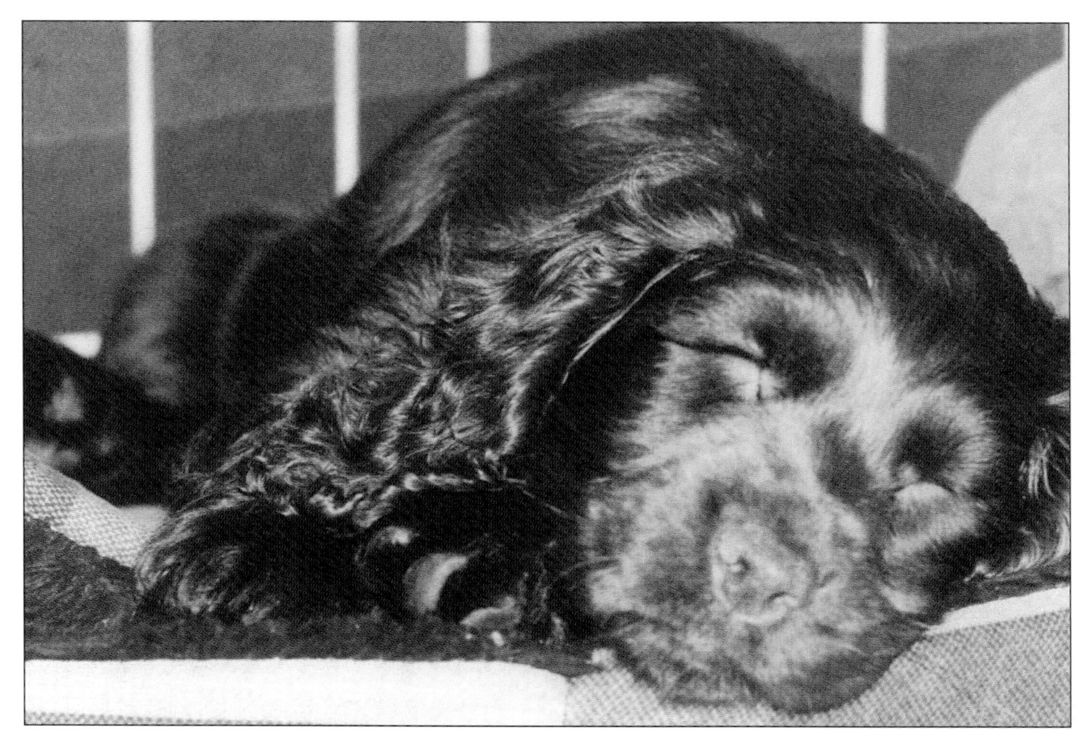

14 The puppy Kestrel dreams of future forays

15 *A group of Hedley's puppies being introduced to the water*

16 Jill contemplates the wonders of winter

17 Hedley and Ian Robertson on the Scottish moors

18 Getting to know Trista Seafoam

19 Beryl Chappell's painting of Hedley and his Nancarrow champions

20 *Heading for lunch after a good morning's work*

Rank heather is in my opinion as tough as any cover, tougher than most, including heavy bramble. When it's literally full of rabbits then it's a spaniel's paradise.

All that basic steadiness training is now put to the test for the younger dogs – the first year entry – that you take with you. It also quite literally tunes up the experienced dogs ready for the coming season.

All of them become exceptionally fit during these forays. To see them emerging from the heather with their noses grey with pollen is a joy.

I usually take six to eight dogs with me, so an investment in a purpose-built dog trailer I made some years ago ensures that they travel and overnight in great comfort. I just load them up and head north for the Border country, then further north to Perth.

We spend much of our time on a sporting estate where I go out with my old friend Bobby Clark. He enjoys shooting over my cockers and I appreciate working them to a superb shot. I simply do not have to concern myself with the shooting and I can concentrate 100% on dog work.

I take four dogs out in the morning and work one while a friend holds the other three on the lead. Then I ring the changes as and when the dogs start to blow. And blow they do when they've worked the heather for a while. It really is formidable stuff.

I tend to work younger dogs on ground with fewer rabbits, perhaps a flush every 15 or 20 yards. The older, more experienced dogs I take into the thick of the action where you'll get multiples of rabbits bursting from the one flush.

The advantages are obvious – steadiness and the polishing up of retrieving skills – because cockers never get bored of picking up rabbits and it is the right situation to teach younger dogs to release the quarry if they happen to 'peg' a rabbit.

That evokes memories of a great battle of wills among the heather with my bitch Pebble.

She grabbed a rabbit in the heather and I told her to leave it. She wouldn't at first, then I ordered her more sternly 'Leave it.'

Pebble let the rabbit go and it moved just a pace away from her before she crept on and put her paw over it! I gave the command again and this time she put her head over the rabbit.

Pebble relented in the end and I had my way, but that was the turning point in my relationship with one of the most talented but potentially wilful cockers I ever had the pleasure to handle.

She went on to become F.T. Ch. Bournepark Blaze of Nancarrow and I think Pebble and I owed that achievement in no small part to the Scottish training regime among the heather.

Another great experience was with my lovely bitch Ronda. I took her goose flighting and was privileged to watch an astonishing red sunrise over an estuary, then hear the sound of two thousand geese rising.

We were stationed behind a hedge line when the guide called in a group and I took the only bird out of the party.

My neighbour looked at my little dog and volunteered his Labrador for the task of picking, but I shook my head saying, 'My bird, my dog thank you'.

I sent Ronda back and she stopped dead in her tracks five yards from the bird. She had never had a close up of a goose before and looked back to me as if to say 'What the hell's that?'

'Fetch it!' I shouted, whereupon she leapt the last few yards to collect the bird and make a perfect retrieve.

I'd seen the sunrise, I had shot and watched my dog pull off a great retrieve. What could have been better? I bade my fellows a good morning and left the flight line so that nothing could take the magic off an experience that lives with me to this day.

CHAPTER FIVE

A right royal to-do

Cockers are great social levellers; no respecters of titles or wealth are these little dogs. The only power they recognise has to do with rough cover, while the only wealth they know is the joy of hunting.

Their very independence ensures that the cocker spaniel is a breed much sort after by the rich and powerful, and my association with cockers has introduced me to the great and the good of the land, most of them proper toffs, some royalty.

It was cockers who introduced me to the Queen herself in a close encounter of a very unusual kind. I can say that with little fear of contradiction, as I know of no other in the land who has had a heart attack in Her Majesty's company and lived to tell the tale. But more of that later.

I admire the Royal family for their knowledge and understanding of animals, and for the obvious respect they show them. I believe they are country folk through and through and I have little doubt that their hearts are in that country.

In the encounters I've had with royalty their devotion to dogs has been a sight to admire. Trialling folk, of course, need no telling of the Queen's fantastic support for all the working breeds in her realm.

Princess Anne, too, has been a stalwart of trials and tests and has made it her business to re-establish the clumber as a sound working breed, in honour, I believe, of her great grandfather, King George V.

Some years ago I ran my chocolate dog Snipe – my pride and joy – in a rabbit trial on a Suffolk estate belonging to Sir Joshua Rolley. Snipe was running in an all aged any variety rabbit stake.

Snipe was brilliant on rabbits and went well through the bracken that day. Sir Joshua, who was Lord Lieutenant of the County, watched Snipe on both his runs and seemed impressed.

He asked me if I'd kindly stay on with my dog and let him shoot a few rabbits over Snipe. Well, it was a pleasure to do so with a man who knew what he was doing and was enjoying his sport. We went on and shot a few rabbits and at the end of the day he thanked me for the experience. I bade him farewell and thought no more of it.

Later in the season I qualified Snipe for the cocker championship to be held at Sandringham in the presence of Her Majesty the Queen.

I was further along the line, but saw the Queen in the distance, together with Sir Joshua. He was pointing towards Snipe with a stick, and eventually the Queen moved along the line to stand directly behind me.

On these occasions the handler's wife is allowed into the line to watch her husband's dog work. Audrey, my wife at the time, was behind me when she got a tap on the shoulder from Bill Meldrum, the Queen's head keeper, and no finer man in the land.

'Do you mind, could you move over Audrey?' asked Bill.

'Bugger off Bill,' she replied forthrightly, 'I'm watching Hedley.'

Another tap on the shoulder and Bill asked coyly 'Do you mind Audrey, the Queen would like to see.'

We thought that amusing, but more was to follow.

Her Majesty watched Snipe in his first run, then came to watch him in the run off with six other dogs.

Here again the Queen showed her mettle when she came to a plank bridge across to an island where the trial had progressed. It crossed my mind that the anything but permanent-looking plank bridge would have given a hardened sapper second thoughts. But the Queen called up Bill and asked 'Is the bridge safe?'

'Yes ma'am,' came the reply. With that the Queen walked across, with her shepherds' crook in the air. The look of triumph was unmistakable.

Her two ladies-in-waiting were more circumspect and hung back until the Queen spotted them and called them over.

It was a joy to see the Queen of the country so relaxed, enjoying the dog work and in her element. I wish her detractors could see her as we in the trialling fraternity do.

At this point Snipe commenced the run off. A duck had been shot and three dogs had been called up to retrieve it and, apparently, all had failed.

The Queen was admiring Snipe, but by now, although I didn't realise it, I was in the process of beginning a heart attack.

Her majesty was still talking to me. 'What a magnificent head he has,' she said.

'Yes ma'am,' I replied. We now knew that the other dogs had failed the water and she asked 'Do all cockers fail the water, Mr Millington?'

'He won't ma'am.' By this time my sight was failing, but I was desperate to finish the championship. I asked Dennis Douglas, the judge, where the duck was.

He pointed in a vague direction and I simply said to old Snipe 'Fetch', and gestured in the direction Dennis had indicated. He disappeared and I remember he was gone for several minutes.

Then he appeared with a duck in his mouth close to the bank where the Queen and I stood. I was very proud of him. I remember taking the duck from his mouth, and then walking a few yards.

The next thing I remember is waking up in hospital in King's Lynn the following day.

I'd had a heart attack bang in front of the Queen and to this day I don't know what the etiquette is for a right royal thrombosis. Perhaps you should bow before you fall. I don't suppose it's something her courtiers have much call for.

The real lesson comes in the sequel, in the attention and care shown me by the royal household. The comptroller of the Queen's household rang me in hospital on several occasions to see how I was.

She also rang to say that she'd heard I had dogs billeted in the car and would I like them to be cared for in the Queen's kennels, something that was done for the duration of my illness.

Another encounter with royalty was on an informal shoot on Duchy land where I was given the honour of picking up for Prince Charles, with my old dog Ronda.

The Prince took one look at her and asked, with some doubt, 'Can she pick a full grown pheasant?'

'No problem sir,' I replied, 'she has picked up hare and geese before now.'

The disbelief that crept across the Prince's face gave me an inner chuckle. 'You shoot one for her sir.'

The Prince is a magnificent shot and a great sportsman. That morning there were not so many birds about and he let some go that were not high enough.

Then he shot a fine high cock pheasant, handed the gun to the gentleman with him and stood back to watch Ronda.

I simply said to her 'Fetch.' She whizzed out, was in the brambles for a few minutes, eventually emerging from the right, a big cock pheasant in her mouth. Head held high, feathers trailing on the ground, she was coming back to me as proud as punch.

HRH smiled. 'I think you two had better stay with me all day.'

Another facet of the Prince's character emerged later that same day. While we broke for coffee I asked a favour of him.

I had a very good friend in Jo Rickards, a cocker-mad society lady. When I needed an urgent quadruple heart bypass operation, Jo had organised a collection among her many friends to enable me to bypass the National Health waiting list. Some of those people were friends of mine too, friends made through cockers.

I believe Jo saved my life by her actions, but now she was in grave trouble with cancer herself.

As the Prince and I took coffee I mentioned this to him. 'Oh yes, one of Colonel Roberts' daughters.'

'Yes sir.'

'Where is Mrs Rickards now?' he asked.

I told him and his detective took down her address. We concluded a nice day out and that was that.

By now Jo was very ill indeed, but a few days later she rang in jovial mood to say 'Guess what?'

She had received a six-page hand-written letter from the Prince wishing her well, hoping things would improve and retelling anecdotes concerning her father.

In recent years the Prince has been heavily criticised for this and that, but in my book a man in his position who writes six pages by hand to a woman on the brink is a man with compassion.

Some time later I was with Lady Tryon, another friendship formed through a mutual love of cockers.

It was around the time that the Prince had lost his terrier Pooh. I told Lady Tryon how sorry I felt about him losing his dog. I said I would like to write and offer him a cocker puppy. 'What's stopping you Hedley?' she enquired.

'The letter would never get to him,' I replied.

'If you give it to me I will make sure it does,' she said, and so it did.

Prince Charles' reply arrived in a few days, thanking me for my concern and explaining that he didn't think he could handle a cocker and instead was getting another terrier from the same line as Pooh.

As a loyal Englishman I wish all the Royals well. And let none of us forget what great servants and ambassadors of our country, country life and pursuits they are.

By the way, after I'd put Snipe out through my faint heart, and through no fault of his own, my old friend Cyril Gwynne from Wales went on to win that championship at Sandringham.

CHAPTER SIX

Trials and tribulations

While I have had my successes at trials, it is some of the crueller twists of the tail, so to speak, that bring a smile to my face when recalling them.

I was running Migdale Ben, a black cocker with a white bib, at the Bleasdale championship judged by Harry Hardwicke.

Ben was a sensitive lad. You couldn't shout at him, but if you asked Ben to do something he would do his best to please. He handled well and had no real vices.

On this particular and important day he'd worked quite well in his first run. A dog to our right had failed on a woodcock, but being Cornish Ben was well used to them, more or less reared on them.

He found the woodcock, no problem, and eye-wiped the other dog. We finished this particular piece of cover and Harry turned and said 'put your dog on the lead and follow me'.

We came over a ride in the woods and walked along to set up and start a forward line. Everything was fine until I happened to gaze down at Ben and saw he had a hen pheasant in his mouth. I just couldn't believe it. There we were in the middle of the championship and he'd actually picked up this bird whilst on the lead!

I told Ben to leave it. He let go of the bird, which then walked quietly over to a very small piece of upright bracken, the only piece standing all around us.

Harry turned to me and said 'Right, away you go.' Before I started I left my dog sat and went over to the bracken and flattened every piece with my foot. No bird. It had vanished.

I flattened the bracken again for good measure. Satisfied, I walked back and started my dog off. He went to the right, back to the left, right again and then left to the bracken that I had just steam-rolled, pushed his nose right underneath and pulled out the hen pheasant.

I told him to leave it, with no effect whatsoever. He brought it right back to me in a very neat retrieve. Harry took the bird, held it in his hand before the bird flew off. With it went my chances in the championship for another year.

Ah well, back to the drawing board. As I put Ben on the lead I swear there was a devilish glint to his eye.

Another amusing incident, although it might not have been for a novice handler, happened whilst I was in Scotland running two field trial champions who needed a first place to qualify for the championship.

Both dogs ran superbly well on the day. I would have had difficulty separating them. Snipe was superb and Bunterson ran brilliantly too.

A good friend was stewarding for the judge and told me 'You've got first and second Hedley.'

'Well,' I said ' Let's put it this way. I am in Scotland, so I'll wait and see.'

Sure enough, just before the announcement, a very well known judge in Scotland pulled me to one side.

'Hadlee,' he said in his fine northern brogue 'you should be first with your chocolate dog. You are. You should be second with your black dog, but you're not. I'm having no Englishman come up here and take first and second in my trial.'

It rather amused me. As predicted Snipe was first and my black dog was placed fourth. I had the last laugh, however, as the following day I ran Bunterson in another trial which he won, so qualifying for the championship as well.

Perhaps the strangest occasion of all, though, was the only time I ever refused a retrieve in a trial.

It was at Windsor Great Park and the trial moved close to the edge of a large enclosure, somewhat similar to a fenced deer park.

A cock pheasant was shot by one of the guns and landed on the other side of the fencing, within full sight. But there was no way that I was going to send my dog and it wasn't the substantial obstacle of the fence that was worrying me.

It was the two or three hard-mouthed canines waiting to pick up – with very clear ideas of how they would eye-wipe my dog – which worried me.

I told the judge 'If you want that bird you go and get it yourself.' He assessed the situation and decided this was probably the one bird in the one trial he would leave.

You see the bird had fallen behind a high fence keeping the wolves in their enclosure at Windsor Safari Park adjoining the shoot. A few of the inhabitants were already circling their supper!

21 *With Tumble at the Tyne Tees and Tweed field trial*

22 *Nancarrow Bernie, owned by Cornish farmer Caladin Phillips, entertains a new-found friend*

23 *Working cocker develops a working relationship with tawny and little owl*

24 Hedley with special friend Tumble in the kitchen at Nancarrow

25 Robin and Henrietta, the Duke and Duchess of Bedford, on a visit to Nancarrow

26 Robin discusses eating arrangements with Millie in the Woburn Abbey kitchens

27 *Mature female peregrine falcon in training for work with cockers*

28 Jill Notley puts a trainee through the poles

29 Hedley and Kathy repair to the Cornish Arms at Frogpool after their wedding in August 1997

30 Blackie, the politically incorrect cocker who helped the Wiltshire police force right a lot of wrongs

CHAPTER SEVEN

Healing friends

Life took on a dark side a few years after I settled in Cornwall in 1964. I woke up one morning to find a hard lump in my groin. I made an appointment to see the doctor. It was just before Christmas 1968, and I remember it as if it were yesterday.

My GP sent me straight to hospital where the lump was removed for a biopsy. The result came back. I had Hodgkin's Disease, a form of cancer. I would require radiotherapy at Freedom Fields Hospital in Plymouth, and they wanted me in straight away.

All the main shoots on Lord Falmouth's estate are clustered around Christmas and I couldn't let the man down. I said nothing.

When we had finished all the main shoots I went back to hospital, had the stitches removed and continued with my treatment and radiotherapy in Plymouth.

That was followed by various operations over the years: lymph glands taken off the liver, lymph glands taken from my neck, many doses of chemotherapy and of radiation.

What does this have to do with cocker spaniels, you might ask?

At the time a wonderful specialist called Matthew Fenner was treating me. We became very great friends. We chatted about dogs and country sports and eventually he and I would go out together in the field.

He liked to relax away from the hospital and the strains of work by going out with the dogs and me, he to do a little shooting, I the dog work. It was all very relaxed and we built up a strong bond.

There followed several years of treatment by knife and chemicals. I finally shook off the illness in the late 1970s.

I found one of the biggest problems with cancer is depression, long bouts when you become moody, bad-tempered and irritable. It was like sitting on a time bomb waiting for the next explosion.

Ultimately I was lucky. I was cured and I can sympathise with anyone who suffers or has suffered with cancer. It beleaguers the spirit as well as the body.

During periods of illness when I was really depressed I would take two or three of my little cockers on a walk. I'd disappear under a hedge with them, talk with them, just be with them.

The therapy I derived from them was astonishing. It was almost as though they sensed my moods, something I found really healing. It's beyond me to explain, but it was a wonderful feeling.

Anyone with healing problems who loves animals should lean on them. The love they give you is a life-giving tonic in itself.

I would just talk out my problems with dogs. And the bond between us made life so much more understandable.

A desperately sad postcript to all this is that Matthew Fenner, the man who had helped me through my ordeal, died some 20 years ago of the very same complaint that he cured in me. What a brave man, treating other people for an illness he knew he was suffering himself.

The only consolation I can take from this is that I know what a pleasure he drew from those simple rough shooting and pottering days he had with me.

I know in my heart that my little dogs gave him that same unspoken and inexplicable comfort they gave me. If only the outcome had been different.

I've seen this healing help in others too.

I sold a blue roan cocker named Jamie to Marjorie, wife of Captain Crook of Somerset. Marjorie was suffering from Hodgkin's and she and Jamie were inseparable. She later told me that he helped give her the strength to beat her problem.

Another resident at the Crook residence at that time was a tame crow called Jim, who followed the captain everywhere. Jim used to watch as shallots and onions were planted, then when all was clear he'd hop along and dig them up.

Jim was fed on raw mince rolled into little balls. If there were any left after he had eaten his fill, he would hide them in a dry stone wall. Then Jamie, who had a nose for such things, would sniff out these tasty morsels. Jim showed his fury by landing on Jamie's back and tugging out pieces of hair, but Jamie seemed to enjoy this and took little notice!

Another time Jo Rickards told me of an army captain who was severely disabled in a crash while returning from an exercise. She asked me if I had a suitable cocker for him, so we gave him one called Sky.

Sky and the captain bonded immediately, the cocker providing hours of company and solace when all his helpers went home in the evening. Another great success for cocker therapy.

I have taken my cockers into the old people's ward at the local hospital and watched the transformation they have brought to the room. I have seen severely withdrawn people come alive in such situations, tears running down their face as they ask about the dogs, then reminiscing about dogs they owned and loved when they were more able.

My bitch Ronda soon got to know the drill and which pensioners would give her her favourite sweets.

Don't ask me to explain this phenomenon, but I have witnessed the power of animal therapy first hand. I experienced it when I was at my lowest ebb, I know it is there and I know it can work the most extraordinary miracles.

I am not a particularly religious man, but I firmly believe that God put dogs on earth to give man a greater understanding of animals. They are the perfect example of love and affection.

I just put it down to one of nature's wonders. Perhaps it has its roots in the distant days when our forbears first domesticated the wild dogs that followed them at a distance when they hunted.

Eventually, in the early 1980s, I was reluctantly forced to retire from my service with Lord Falmouth. My health was that bad.

There I was, a man of few means, a sick gamekeeper with a dozen dogs and not prepared to part with one of them. Where could I go, what could I do?

Lord Falmouth came to the rescue and offered me premises out at Bissoe in 1982, where I later set up Nancarrow Kennels. It was a kindness by his lordship for which I will be eternally grateful.

It proved the turning point for me.

CHAPTER EIGHT

Adaptable

The great thing about working bred dogs of all sorts is their ability to adapt to new roles in the service of man. Hence we see many different roles carved out by various breeds, from guide dogs at the turn of the century to explosives dogs in our current troubled times.

It wasn't long before the newly resurgent working cocker drew attention to himself from people who could use and adapt his skills they had traditionally used in the shooting field.

So it was that in the late 1980s I sold the first working cocker used for drug work to the Wiltshire police force in Devizes. They were particularly interested in his size and agility in getting into tight corners not even his larger spaniel cousin, the springer, could negotiate.

He was a dog called Blackie and he was an immediate success, a great favourite at headquarters. He later went on to do a great deal of PR work for the police.

Blackie was a real character. Once he accompanied his handler across a building site, stopped and immediately dug up a purse full of money obviously buried by a criminal to be recovered later.

On another occasion police stopped two new age travellers after one of them had hurled something into a cornfield alongside the road. The police search found nothing, but then they called for Blackie who quickly found a container full of cannabis.

Unfortunately, after retrieving the illicit goods he decided to swallow the lot. The police waited two nervous days before their evidence reappeared. Well, even Sherlock Holmes had his bad days!

Then I heard that the head of the dog section had been called in to see the top brass over Blackie. A coloured officer had joined the force, he was told, and there were to be no more dogs bearing the unfortunate name of Blackie, even though a perfectly accurate description of the dog.

I have many friends of different colours and creeds and this gave me a good laugh. I promptly celebrated this piece of politically correct nonsense by naming my next black dog Whitie.

By now cockers were in demand as drugs and explosives dogs and I received a visit from a charming man who was the chief superintendent in the Jamaican police.

They were and still are desperately trying to curb the drug problem dragging their society down and were looking for a new weapon to use against the dealers.

The chief superintendent had been sent on a recommendation to see my dogs and I gave him a demonstration of the working abilities of a cocker. I shall always remember the officer, for he was a very big and powerfully built man and he had to stand between the beams in my cottage.

We went out to a rabbit pen where he asked if my dog could retrieve a small dummy he held in his hand. The weather was awful, it was raining very hard and my dog Snipe was quartering his ground when the dummy was thrown. Snipe duly retrieved it.

I was then asked if he could retrieve the dummy if he hadn't seen it. The dummy was hidden, but Snipe found it easily.

The officer's next question was more interesting. If he buried the object would the dog still find it? I told him I didn't know, but that I was prepared to give it a go.

He buried the dummy in a disused rabbit hole before filing the hole in. Snipe was then worked out to the hedge and along it, scratched out the hole, found the dummy and brought it to my hand.

The chief superintendent said 'I'm very impressed.' I didn't tell him so there and then, but I was very impressed too! The result was that the British government bought several dogs from me for the Jamaican police force where I presume their off-spring are still fighting the war on drugs.

CHAPTER NINE

The Texans are coming

I once met a young man who came to my kennels to ask if he could use my rabbit pen to train his dog.

'No,' I replied bluntly.

'What if I paid you?' he enquired.

'No, I don't need it.'

Showing persistence and determination he asked 'Well, what if I cut your grass?'

'Ah, that's better. Well, you can cut the grass and then you can use the rabbit pen.'

His attitude showed me what I wanted to see, a young man keen to work to achieve what he wanted. This was the start of a good friendship with Martin Bell who at the age of 29 was about to become one of America's top trial handlers.

Martin and I went everywhere together, training dogs in Scotland in the heather and rushes until eventually he moved to Texas to further his career. There he met Shelley, the Texan girl he was to marry, and opened kennels at Shelmar in Katy, near Houston.

Martin wrote from time to time, keeping me up to date on the success of the dogs I had exported to America. Two of the most successful were F.T.Ch. Nancarrow Rosy Mantle and F.T.Ch. Nancarrow Golden Echo. Rosy produced eleven puppies in two litters, of which eight were destined to become American field trial champions.

Late on in 2002, completely out of the blue, I received an invitation to judge the first cocker trials in Texas. Being utterly disillusioned by the atmosphere at British trials, I thought long and hard about accepting. Also, having had two heart attacks, a quadruple by-pass and two new knees, I had thought I would retire from such matters with just my memories.

Also, I couldn't get out of my head some of the things I had heard over the years concerning American trials – rubbish dogs, ignorant handlers and the rest. How wrong those misconceptions would turn out to be, more of which later.

A mixture of stubbornness, intrigue and curiosity got the better of me, however, so in January last year Kathy and I set off on the long haul from Newquay Airport through Gatwick to Houston where we were met by Shelley and driven to Katy.

Texans tell you that their state is big. No, it's enormous. It is also noticeably flat, especially for someone bought up on the heather moors of my native Yorkshire and the splendid rolling hills of my adopted Cornwall. Thousands of acres of flat Texan countryside are flooded for the purpose of growing rice, which in turn has created a wonderful environment for wildlife: thousands of geese, many species of duck, waders of every type and birds of prey I didn't know existed. And to go with this diverse range of wildlife they have had the good sense to introduce rigidly enforced, strictly controlled conservation laws that limit the amount of game and wild fowl that may be shot.

From what I saw this works very well. There's none of the mass slaughter, huge bags so beloved of too many people here in Britain where greed rules far too often.

We saw racoons, possums, armadillo, many species of deer, and we smelt skunk (not recommended). We were warned to look out for rattlesnakes and copperheads and when we went training Martin showed us a pool into which an alligator had recently moved, so making it off limits. We didn't see it, or the snakes, but we took Martin's word!

We spent one evening in the company of John Kelsey, commissioner for wildlife in Texas. John has a wealth of experience, is a keen shooting and dog man with a real love of wildlife.

I went training with the American lads to see their methods. I say American as opposed to Texan because they come from all over the States, thinking nothing of travelling thousands of miles to compete. I found this very therapeutic, like travelling backwards in a time warp to a Britain twenty-five years ago when people trialled for the love of being able to work their dogs, not for monetary gain. If these people are true Americans, then God bless America.

What impressed me is the high standard and quality of the dogs and I felt proud that a number of Nancarrow dogs had helped form the nucleus. I don't think they need any more help with the breeding as I saw dogs that I would like to have brought home. One particular owner whose dog, a little cocker called Trouble, had just been made into an American F.T.Ch. by Martin Bell, dashed off to show Trouble what she had just won, which is just typical of the love and care of dogs shown by these people.

CHAPTER TEN

The future

So what does the future hold for the cocker? Well, I have mixed feelings on the subject.

For one thing, some of the finest friends of the breed are being driven out by back-biting, politicking and unsportsmanlike behaviour among the cocker trialling fraternity.

My old friend Cyril Gwynne, a champions' champion and one of the kindest and most honest men you could wish to meet, has washed his hands of the breed and turned to sheepdog trialling for more sporting companionship.

But what is equally worrying is the future of the breeding of the cocker. I have publicly warned of the dangers we face on more than one occasion, but I feel that I am old enough and daft enough to speak my mind.

I know that younger men who hope to make an impact in the trialling world agree with the views I'm about to put forward, but are keeping quiet because they fear the sport's establishment, the 'powers that be', will turn their guns on them and literally ruin their chances.

Since the 1970s when my old friend Peter Moxon – an arch 'cocker knocker' – quite rightly rubbished the breed as it was then, we have made great strides, Nowadays the little pocket rockets are seen more and more in the beating line and picking up on shoots all over Britain.

Even as the likes of Cyril Gwynne, Peter Jones and Dennis Douglas and myself were striving to bring the breed out of the doldrums, troubles were already brewing. And the trouble is in the breeding.

It was in the late 1980s that I first voiced my disquiet about cocker breeding. Certain lines were being developed with an illicit dash of springer blood in the mistaken belief that it would give the cocker a harder hunting quality.

The result is there for all to see and far too common now. The sprocker is alive and well and a hollow joke on the breed I love.

The sprocker's size, his gait and action all give the lie to their stolen title of cocker and these impostors are a blight on the breed.

The true cocker is bold and courageous in cover, it'll hunt as hard as any dog in my opinion and has better scenting ability than the springer. Its diminutive size too can be a winner in the tightest of corners, the narrowest of cracks in a tree trunk or even finding a runner down a rabbit hole.

The cocker never needed an injection of springer, something perpetrated by quick-fix gun dog breeders whose heart was not with the breed but whose hands were firmly on their wallets.

That's how it started, but if breeders created the virus, then it's the judge's who have nurtured it and spread it.

For the truth is that the majority of qualified spaniel judges are springer men and wouldn't have a cocker in the kennel.

What a vindication for them then, while judging a cocker stake, to see, lo and behold, a dog they like the look of turning out on parade. Little wonder they have favoured so-called cockers with the action and style they prefer – that of a springer!

They have progressed these impostors with awards and placings they should never have been given.

When I first raised these issues I was more or less ostracised by many of my companions, but now the Cocker Club has at least acknowledged it exists.

The solution must lie with the professional. The shooting man who fancies a spaniel to enhance his pleasure in his sport won't even be aware of the problem.

But professional breeders know about it all too well and it is they who must start to ruthlessly avoid the lines involved and to avoid working and breeding from suspect stock. Only then can we begin to protect the true cocker.

It's a bleak picture, because we have been cheated and straightforward cheating it is. What would springer lovers think if one of their top breeders sneaked in a dash of Labrador to beef up the long distance retrieving abilities of the breed so that he looked good in a trial? Not a lot, I suspect.

It is not right. The cocker has qualities all of his own, as does the springer. I happen to like the smaller spaniel. Why should shallow men whose hearts are in their pockets cheat me?

There should also be a complete overhaul of the cocker championships. It should be a separate event run by the breeds own club under the Kennel Club, not an afterthought for a second class citizen.

It should be a two day event like the springers have and it should be judged by cocker specialists, not by springer enthusiasts, some of whom can barely hide their disdain for cockers.

For all that I have said I still believe the cocker will beat all cheats. After all, the breed was moribund for decades until it was revived in more recent years.

Now it has powerful allies on some of the great sporting estates in the land and a growing band of adoring fans that like me are hooked on its sparkling action.

Above all else, quality will out, and the cocker has that by the gallon. I'm confident true cocker men and women will win the day.

CHAPTER ELEVEN

Choosing your puppy . . . and early care

Just looking at a seven or eight week old puppy is not going to give you enough clues as to his or her future potential. So before you arrive at this stage you should study various cocker pedigrees to satisfy yourself that the pup you are considering is bred on sound working lines.

Now that you have done your homework, establish that everyone in the household wants this puppy. If they do, then the puppy is going to a good home.

The next decision is dog or bitch?

Personally, I seem to bond better with a bitch, but then again I have had some superb dogs.

If you decide on a bitch, and you are not going to breed from her, then at some stage after her first full season you should have her spayed. Apart from other considerations, like unwanted pregnancies, you will not have the problem of her being continually pursued by dogs. It can also eliminate the problem of mammary tumours in her later life.

One misconception regarding spaying is that a bitch will automatically become dull and overweight, but this is easily avoided through correct diet and exercise.

Having a bitch spayed will not in any way affect her desire to hunt.

If you are going to look at puppies where they have been bred and reared, do not be overly influenced by what the breeder is telling you. Use your own judgement to identify the condition – sleek coat, clear eyes, lively – and ability of the puppies.

Look for the puppy that seems bold and confident, the one that approaches without signs of fear. Put your hand down near the ground and see which one is really curious.

You could take along a pheasant or duck wing, even a rabbit's foot, to discover the pup's interest in retrieving this. Most puppies of the right breeding will willingly pick up and carry these objects. They may not bring the object to hand, but to run and play with it is not a fault. If the puppy picks it up and brings it to you, though, then you are definitely on the right lines.

To reject the smallest pup for no other reason than its size can be a mistake. If it's small, healthy and bright, then it has clearly overcome its shortcomings and exhibited strength of mind in making sure it got his or her share of mother's milk and other food.

I am not advocating that you automatically choose the smallest one, merely that you should not dismiss it.

You should insist on seeing the dam and sire, or the papers that show that their eyes were tested for the hereditary condition progressive retinal atrophy. Also make sure your puppy has had a strict worming plan and when the next worming is due.

Once the puppy is yours and you have him home, you should waste no time in getting the puppy to your vet, who will give them a full examination and all the necessary vaccinations so vital to the puppy's welfare.

Tail docking and dewclaw removal are essential. A working dog's tail should not be docked as short as a show dog's. Only one third of the tail should be removed by a veterinary surgeon, enabling the dog to cover his or her genitals, but still long enough to indicate by tail movement when he is in the vicinity of game.

If the tail of a hard working cocker is kept undocked this can cause serious damage to the tip, resulting in a general anaesthetic to remove the damaged part.

Modern dog feeding is very simple, as there are so many good brands of puppy food on the market, so find out from the breeder which one and what method he has used and continue with that one. This way you will help avoid tummy upsets.

Puppies are usually fed four times a day. I advocate letting him eat his fill as it helps to form good bone and muscle, and any excess will be burnt off by his constant physical activity!

Remember he only has a small stomach, so what goes in must be of good quality.

From five months old you should cut his feeds down to two a day, and from nine months old to one a day. The only bone I recommend is marrowbone, and never ever feed a bone which can splinter.

CHAPTER TWELVE

Secrets of success

Follow these golden rules of training a young dog and you won't go far wrong.

1. It is only impossible until you do it.
2. Never overdo a lesson and bore the puppy.
3. Always make your puppy succeed, even if you have to go back a lesson.
4. A happy pup will always want to learn more.
5. Combine your lessons with something your puppy enjoys, such as taking a walk or playing in the yard.
6. Never move on to the next lesson until you have perfected the previous one.
7. Always be consistent with pup.

8. Five minutes a day, five days a week, for four months will save a ten-year mistake.
9. Repetition, repetition, repetition.
10. Always firm, always fair.
11. Never, ever lose your temper.
12. Playtime is as important as training time.
13. All training should be kept short and sweet.
14. Make haste slowly.
15. Start small and work your way up to greater things.
16. It will work if you practice and give it time.
17. Always end training sessions on a good note.
18. Keep distractions to a minimum in early stages of training.
19. All commands are soft and reassuring in early stages, never shouted.
20. Never pressure your pup into learning too fast, take each step as it comes.
21. Success is learnt, not born or bred.
22. 90% trainer, 10% dog.
23. Success = confidence.
24. Confidence = greater success.

31 Scamp, Hedley and Pebble

32 *Jill Notley's Rawnee, bred at Nancarrow, taking – and passing – her agility test*

33 F.T. Ch. Nancarrow Gypsy

34 *Pebble, painted by Beryl Chappell*

35 Nancarrow Star

36 *F.T. Ch. Heathill Lad*

37 *Martin Bell, Hedley and Jim Carvarelt in Texas*

38 *Heathill Lad, another Nancarrow star*

39 F.T. Ch. Wernffrwd Enfys (Welsh for Rainbow), better known as Kate

Five generation pedigree records

FIVE GENERATION PEDIGREE

Breed	COCKER SPANIEL	Breeder	MR H MILLINGTON	Date of Birth	23 -9-1979
Name of Dog	FTCH NANCARROW GYPSY			Date of Registration	
Pet Name				KC Registration No	3543BP
Colour	BLACK & WHITE	Owner	MR H MILLINGTON		
Sex	BITCH				

PARENTS	GRAND-PARENTS	GREAT-GRAND-PARENTS	GT-GREAT-GRAND-PARENTS	GT-GT-GREAT-GRAND-PARENTS
Sire BURNHATCH BRIG	*Sire* CONCRAIG TEAL (FTCH) 1385BI	*Sire* JORDIELAND SPOIT	*Sire* LANEGATE SPOT	*Sire* GEARSTONES FLYOVER
				Dam BRIGHT OF ELAN
			Dam JORDIELAND MUFF	*Sire* GHILLIE OF NETHERMILN
				Dam JORDIELAND JESSIE
		Dam JORDIELAND LASSIE	*Sire* JACK OF WARDRUM	*Sire* SPARKY OF MILLARIES
				Dam MITZIE OF BORELAND
			Dam BELLFIELD SPANGLES	*Sire* JORDIELAND JIM
				Dam SPECLES OF ELAN
	Dam BURNHATCH FLY (FTCH) 0702BF	*Sire* TEMPLEBAR BLACKIE (FTCH)	*Sire* WILFRED OF CROMLIX (FTCH)	*Sire* MERLIN MICKY
				Dam NIX OF CROMLIX
			Dam JET OF ELAN (FTCH)	*Sire* BROOKVILLE SANDY
				Dam GEM OF ELAN
		Dam TEMPLEBAR TANYA	*Sire* DEBDENHALL GEORDIE	*Sire* BUOY OF ELAN (FTCH)
				Dam MAYBELLE
			Dam DEBDENHALL SALLY	*Sire* DEBDENHALL TIMOTHY
K.C. Reg No B12				*Dam* STOCKBURY JILL
Dam MORBORNE TEL	*Sire* HARPERSBROOK SOBERS 074183/69	*Sire* EXTON MONTY	*Sire* EXTON DAVID	*Sire* EXTON DARKIE
				Dam DIAMOND OF PLUSH
			Dam EXTON MOUSIE	*Sire* GLENNEWTON JULIUS (FTCH)
				Dam MERLIN MIZ
		Dam EXTON FIZZ	*Sire* BUOY OF ELAN (FTCH)	*Sire* GLENNEWTON BUOY
				Dam GEISHA GIRL OF ELAN
			Dam EXTON FRECKLES	*Sire* EXTON MICKEY
				Dam EXTON JUDY
	Dam MORBORNE SPEY	*Sire* HEADLAND MUTKIN	*Sire* SWIFT OF ELAN	*Sire* SIMON OF ELAN
				Dam BETA OF ELAN
			Dam HEADLAND GINGER QUILL	*Sire* HEADLAND PROFESSOR
				Dam HEADLAND CINNAMON
		Dam MORBORNE JOY	*Sire* GREATFORD DARKIE (FTCH)	*Sire* JAN BOY
				Dam EXTON MOUSIE
			Dam EXTON FROLIC	*Sire* BUOY OF ELAN (FTCH)
K.C. Reg No 0196BL				*Dam* EXTON FRECKLES

FIVE GENERATION PEDIGREE

Breed	COCKER SPANIEL	Breeder	Date of Birth
Name of Dog	FTCH NACARROW SOOTY OF CRAIGIFELLIN	MR H MILLINGTON	Date of Registration
Pet Name			KC Registration No
Colour	BLACK	Owner	
Sex	BITCH	MR H MILLINGTON	

PARENTS	GRAND-PARENTS	GREAT-GRAND-PARENTS	GT-GREAT-GRAND-PARENTS	GT-GT-GREAT-GRAND-PARENTS
Sire BURNHATCH BRIG	Sire CONCRAIG TEAL (FTCH)	Sire JODIELAND SPOIT	Sire LANEGATE SPOT	Sire GEARSTONES FLYOVER
				Dam BRIGHT OF ELAN
			Dam JORDIELAND MOFF	Sire GHILLIE OF NETHERMILN
				Dam JORDIELAND JESSIE
		Dam JORDIELAND LASSIE	Sire JACK OF WARDMUM	Sire SPARKY OF MILLARIES
				Dam MITZIE OF BORELAND
			Dam BELLFIELD SPANGLES	Sire JORDIELAND JIM
				Dam SPECKLES OF ELAN
	Dam BURNHATCH FLY (FTCH)	Sire TEMPLEBAR BLACKIE (FTCH)	Sire WILFRED OF CROMLIX (FTCH)	Sire MERLIN MICKY
				Dam NIX OF CROMLIX
			Dam JET OF ELAN (FTCH)	Sire BROOKVILLE SANDY
				Dam GEM OF ELAN
		Dam TEMPLEBAR TANYA	Sire DEBDENHALL GORRDIE	Sire BUOY OF ELAN (FTCH)
				Dam MAYBELLE
			Dam DEBDENHALL SALLY	Sire DEBDENHALL TIMOTHY
K.C. Reg No				Dam STOCKBURY JILL
Dam GWIBERNANT EBONY OF RAWRETH	Sire JASPER OF GWIBERNANT	Sire WILFRED OF HURRYON	Sire GWIBERNANT CAPCAJOU	Sire TEMPLEBAR BLACKIE (FTCH)
				Dam SPECKLE OF ARDOON
			Dam MONNOW MAYFLY (FTCH)	Sire PINEHAWK ROBB (FTCH)
				Dam HEADLAND HAZEL OF MONNOW
		Dam SKEET OF HARROCK	Sire TEMPLEBAR BLACKIE (FTCH)	Sire WILFRED OF CROMLIX (FTCH)
				Dam JET OF ELAN (FTCH)
			Dam BUMBLE OF YORKE	Sire HEUGH HEAD MAC
				Dam HOLLY OF YORKE
	Dam IMP OF GWIBERNANT	Sire TEMPLEBAR BLACKIE (FTCH)	Sire WILFRED OF CROMLIX (FTCH)	Sire MERLIN MICKY
				Dam NIX OF CROMLIX
			Dam JET OF ELAN (FTCH)	Sire BROOKVILLE SANDY
				Dam GEM OF ELAN
		Dam SPECKLE OF ARDOON	Sire TIRERAGH SILVER STARLIGHT	Sire SIXSHOT OTTO THE OWL
				Dam TIRERAGH HARVEST MOON
			Dam COLLENN OF ELAN	Sire SWIFT OF ELAN
K.C. Reg No				Dam JET OF ELAN (FTCH)

FIVE GENERATION PEDIGREE

Breed	COCKER SPANIEL	Breeder: MR H MILLINGTON	Date of Birth
Name of Dog	FTCH NANCARROW CAROUSEL		Date of Registration
Pet Name			KC Registration No
Colour	BLACK	Owner: MR H MILLINGTON	
Sex	BITCH		

PARENTS	GRAND-PARENTS	GREAT-GRAND-PARENTS	GT-GREAT-GRAND-PARENTS	GT-GT-GREAT-GRAND-PARENTS
Sire HEATHFIELD LAD (FTCH)	*Sire* PICKLEWOOD OAK	*Sire* BUNTER OF JORDIELAND	*Sire* CARSWELL ZERO (FTCH)	*Sire* DANNY OF NORTH STANDEN
				Dam WHISPER OF CORSEWALL (FTCH)
			Dam DAVINIAG OF DUCHRAE	*Sire* WILFRED OF CROMLIX (FTCH)
				Dam TAYBURN BORGIE
		Dam SOOTY OF WIND MILLWOOD	*Sire* JASPER OF GWIBERNANT	*Sire* WILFRED OF HURRYON
				Dam SKEET OF HARROCK
			Dam IMP OF GWIBERNANT	*Sire* TEMPLEBAR BLACKIE (FTCH)
				Dam SPECKLE OF ARDOON
	Dam SPEY OF SPININGLOCH	*Sire* CARSWELL JIMMY	*Sire* JIMMY OF ELAN (FTCH)	*Sire* SWIFT OF ELAN
				Dam JET OF ELAN (FTCH)
			Dam WHISPER OF CORSEWALL	*Sire* GALBRY JORDIELAND PODGE
				Dam GALBRY MONA
		Dam MORBORNE TEL	*Sire* HAPERSBROOK SOBERS	*Sire* EXTON MONTY
				Dam EXTON FIZZ
			Dam MORBORNE SPEY	*Sire* HEADLAND MUTCHKIN
K.C. Reg No				*Dam* MORBORNE JOY
Dam BOURNE PACK BLAZE OF NANCARROW (FTCH)	*Sire* SWALLOW LAW SNIPE (FTCH)	*Sire* SMUT OF JORDIELAND (FTCH)	*Sire* GWIBERNANT EEL (FTCH)	*Sire* GWIBERNANT CAPCAJOU
				Dam MONNOW ELIZABETH
			Dam MONNOW ELIZABETH	*Sire* PINEHAWK ROBB (FTCH)
				Dam HEADLAND HAZEL OF MONNOW
		Dam MISTY LAW KATY	*Sire* MIGDALE BEN OF WEAVERDALE (FTCH)	*Sire* BUNTER OF JORDIELAND (FTCH)
				Dam MIGDALE LIZ
			Dam MEG OF THE MILL	*Sire* RHU OF MIGDALE (FTCH)
				Dam MERRYMAID OF BROXTON
	Dam WERNFFWD PAWN	*Sire* RHU OF MIGDALE (FTCH)	*Sire* SOUTHFIELD SAM	*Sire* ARDAMURCHAN MAC (FTCH)
				Dam VICTORIA OF CORSLEY
			Dam GINGER OF GWIBERNANT	*Sire* ARDOON WILGO
				Dam ARDOON ROMPER
		Dam GWIBERNANT SNAKE (FTCH)	*Sire* JASPER OF GWIBERNANT	*Sire* WILFRED OF HARROCK
				Dam SKEET OF HARROCK
			Dam IMP OF GWIBERNANT	*Sire* TEMPLEBAR BLACKIE (FTCH)
K.C. Reg No				*Dam* SPECKLE OF ARDOON

FIVE GENERATION PEDIGREE

Breed	COCKER SPANIEL	Breeder	Date of Birth
Name of Dog	FTCH SWALLOW LAW SNIPE		Date of Registration
Pet Name			KC Registration No
Colour	CHOCOLATE	Owner	
Sex	DOG	MR H MILLINGTON	

PARENTS	GRAND-PARENTS	GREAT-GRAND-PARENTS	GT-GREAT-GRAND-PARENTS	GT-GT-GREAT-GRAND-PARENTS
Sire SMUT OF JORDIELAND (FTCH)	*Sire* GWIBERNANT EEL (FTCH)	*Sire* GWIBERNANT CAPCAJOU	*Sire* TEMPLEBAR BALCKIE (FTCH)	*Sire* WILFRED OF CROMLIX (FTCH)
				Dam JET OF ELAN (FTCH)
			Dam SPECKLE OF ARDOON	*Sire* TIRERAGH SILVER STARLIGHT
				Dam COLLEEN OF ELAN
		Dam MONNOW ELIZABETH	*Sire* PINEHAWK ROBB (FTCH)	*Sire* SWIFT OF ELAN
				Dam BRIGHT OF ELAN
			Dam HEADLAND HAZEL OF MONNOW	*Sire* BOUY OF ELAN (FTCH)
				Dam HEADLAND BLUE HEN SPIDER
	Dam DACRE JET	*Sire* JORDIELAND TIP	*Sire* CROFTMUIR SIMON	*Sire* CARSWELL WISP
				Dam BLACKLUNAN MATE
			Dam JORDIELAND TWIGGY	*Sire* JORDIELAND SPOT
				Dam JORDIELAND LASSIE
		Dam LUCY FEATHERS	*Sire* BUNTER OF JORDIELAND	*Sire* CARSWELL ZERO (FTCH)
				Dam DAVINIAG OF DUCHRAE
			Dam HELEN OF JORDIELAND	*Sire* JORDIELAND DANTA
K.C. Reg No				*Dam* THORNYDALE GYRL
Dam MISTY LAW KATY	*Sire* MIGDALE BEN OF WEAVERDALE (FTCH)	*Sire* BUNTER OF JORDIELAND	*Sire* CARSWELL ZERO (FTCH)	*Sire* DANNY OF NORTH STANDEN
				Dam WHISPER OF CORSEWALL (FTCH)
			Dam DAVINIAG OF DUCHRAE	*Sire* WILFRED OF CROMLIX (FTCH)
				Dam TAYBURN BORGIE
		Dam MIGDALE LIZ	*Sire* JASPER OF GWIBERNANT	*Sire* WILFRED OF HURRYON
				Dam SKEET OF HARROCK
			Dam GINGER OF GWIBERNANT	*Sire* ARDOON WILGO
				Dam ARDOON ROMPER
	Dam MEG OF THE MILL	*Sire* RHU OF MIGDALE (FTCH)	*Sire* SOUTHFIELD SAM	*Sire* ARDNAMURCHAN MAC (FTCH)
				Dam VICTORIA OF CORSLEY
			Dam GINGER OF GWIBERNANT	*Sire* ARDOON WILGO
				Dam ARDOON ROMPER
		Dam MERRYMAID OF BROXTON	*Sire* CARN-GALVA OF BOSISTOW	*Sire* ARDOON WILGO
				Dam ARDOON ROMPER
			Dam LISA OF BOSISTOW	*Sire* MEREHOUSE JASON
K.C. Reg No				*Dam* MONA OF BOSISTOW

FIVE GENERATION PEDIGREE

Breed	COCKER SPANIEL	Breeder	Date of Birth
Name of Dog	FTCH BOURNE PARK BLAZE OF NANCARROW		Date of Registration
Pet Name			KC Registration No
Colour	CHOCOLATE	Owner MR H MILLINGTON	
Sex	BITCH		

PARENTS	GRAND-PARENTS	GREAT-GRAND-PARENTS	GT-GREAT-GRAND-PARENTS	GT-GT-GREAT-GRAND-PARENTS
Sire SWALLOW LAW SNIPE (FTCH)	Sire SMUT OF JORDIELAND (FTCH)	Sire GWIBERNANT EEL (FTCH)	Sire GWIBERNANT CAPCAJOU	Sire TEMPLEBAR BLACKIE (FTCH)
				Dam SPECKLE OF ARDOON
			Dam MONNOW ELIZABETH	Sire PINEHAWK ROBB (FTCH)
				Dam HEADLAND HAZEL OF MONNOW
		Dam DACRE JET	Sire JORDIELAND TIP	Sire CROFTMUIR SIMON
				Dam JORDIELAND TWIGGY
			Dam LUCY FEATHERS	Sire BUNTER OF JORDIELAND
				Dam HELEN OF JORDIELAND
	Dam MISTY LAW KATY	Sire MIGDALE BEN OF WEAVERDALE (FTCH)	Sire BUNTER OF JORDIELAND (FTCH)	Sire CARSWELL ZERO (FTCH)
				Dam DAVINIAG OF DUCHRAE
			Dam MIGDALE LIZ	Sire JASPER OF GWIBERNANT
				Dam GINGER OF GWIBERNANT
		Dam MEG OF THE MILL	Sire RHU OF MIGDALE (FTCH)	Sire SOUTHFIELD SAM
				Dam GINGER OF GWIBERNANT
			Dam MERRYMAID OF BROXTON	Sire CARN-GALVA OF BOSISTOW
K.C. Reg No				Dam LISA OF BOSISTOW
Dam WERNFFWD PAWN (FTCH)	Sire RHU OF MIGDALE (FTCH)	Sire SOUTHFIELD SAM	Sire ARDAMURCHAN MAC (FTCH)	Sire TEMPLEBAR BLACKIE (FTCH)
				Dam TEMPLEBAR GAIL
			Dam VICTORIA OF CORSLEY	Sire SABLE OF CORSLEY
				Dam EXTON JULIE
		Dam GINGER OF GWIBERNANT	Sire ARDOON WILGO	Sire TIRERAGH SILVER STARLIGHT
				Dam COLLEEN OF ELAN
			Dam ARDOON ROMPER	Sire TEMPLEBAR BLACKIE (FTCH)
				Dam SPECKLE OF ARDOON
	Dam GWIBERNANT SNAKE (FTCH)	Sire JASPER OF GWIBERNANT	Sire WILFRED OF HURRYON	Sire GWIBERNANT CAPCAJOU
				Dam MONNOW MAYFLY
			Dam SKEET OF HARROCK	Sire TEMPLEBAR BLACKIE (FTCH)
				Dam BUMBLE OF YORKE
		Dam IMP OF GWIBERNANT	Sire TEMPLEBAR BLACKIE (FTCH)	Sire WILFRED OF CROMLIX (FTCH)
				Dam JET OF ELAN (FTCH)
			Dam SPECKLE OF ARDOON	Sire TIRERAGH SILVER STARLIGHT
K.C. Reg No				Dam COLLEEN OF ELAN

FIVE GENERATION PEDIGREE

Breed	COCKER SPANIEL	Breeder	Date of Birth
Name of Dog	FTCH WERNFFRWD BUNTERSON		Date of Registration
Pet Name			KC Registration No
Colour	BLACK	Owner	
Sex	DOG	MR H MILLINGTON	

PARENTS	GRAND-PARENTS	GREAT-GRAND-PARENTS	GT-GREAT-GRAND-PARENTS	GT-GT-GREAT-GRAND-PARENTS
Sire BUNTER OF JORDIELAND (FTCH)	Sire CARSWELL ZERO (FTCH)	Sire DANNY OF NORTH STANDEN	Sire JIMMY OF ELAN (FTCH)	Sire SWIFT OF ELAN
				Dam JET OF ELAN (FTCH)
			Dam DAINTY OF LADBROKE	Sire COGIA OF POUGHLEY WOOD
				Dam DINAH OF POUGHLEY WOOD
		Dam WHISPER OF CORSEWALL (FTCH)	Sire GALBRY JORDIELAND PODGE	Sire MERLIN MICKY
				Dam JORDIELAND BUNTY
			Dam GALBRY MONA	Sire GALBRY DANNY BOY
				Dam GALBRY BLONDEYE
	Dam DAVINIAG OF DUCHRAE	Sire WILFRED OF CROMLIX (FTCH)	Sire MERLIN MICKY	Sire GLENNEWTON JULIUS (FTCH)
				Dam MERLIN MIZ
			Dam NIX OF CROMLIX	Sire BOUY OF ELAN
				Dam FRAOCH OF CROMLIX
		Dam TAYBURN BORGIE	Sire SWIFT OF ELAN	Sire SIMON OF ELAN
				Dam BETA OF ELAN
			Dam TAYBURN RHUM	Sire MERLIN MICKY
K.C. Reg No				Dam BRECONHILL DESOMGIRL
Dam GWIBERNANT SNAKE (FTCH)	Sire JASPER OF GWIBERNANT	Sire WILFRED OF HURRYON	Sire GWIBERNANT CAPCAJOU	Sire TEMPLEBAR BLACKIE (FTCH)
				Dam SPECKLE OF ARDOON
			Dam MONNOW MAYFLY	Sire PINEHAWK ROBB (FTCH)
				Dam HEADLAND HAZEL OF MONNOW
		Dam SKEET OF HARROCK	Sire TEMPLEBAR BLACKIE (FTCH)	Sire WILFRED OF CROMLIX (FTCH)
				Dam JET OF ELAN (FTCH)
			Dam BUMBLE OF YORKE	Sire HEUGH HEAD MAC
				Dam HOLLY OF YORKE
	Dam IMP OF GWIBERNANT	Sire TEMPLEBAR BLACKIE (FTCH)	Sire WILFRED OF CROMLIX (FTCH)	Sire MERLIN MICKY
				Dam NIX OF CROMLIX
			Dam JET OF ELAN (FTCH)	Sire BROOKVILLE SANDY
				Dam GEM OF ELAN
		Dam SPECKLE OF ARDOON	Sire TIRERAGH SILVER STARLIGHT	Sire SIXSHOTOTTO THE OWL
				Dam TIRERAGH HARVEST MOON
			Dam COLLEEN OF ELAN	Sire SWIFT OF ELAN
K.C. Reg No				Dam JET OF ELAN (FTCH)

FIVE GENERATION PEDIGREE

Breed	COCKER SPANIEL	Breeder	Date of Birth
Name of Dog	FTCH REGULUSKNOWNE GOLD OF MAESYDDERWEN		Date of Registration
Pet Name			KC Registration No
Colour	LEMON & WHITE	Owner MR H MILLINGTON	
Sex	DOG		

PARENTS	GRAND-PARENTS	GREAT-GRAND-PARENTS	GT-GREAT-GRAND-PARENTS	GT-GT-GREAT-GRAND-PARENTS
Sire MEASYDDERWEN JACKDAW (FTCH)	Sire HOUSTY SOLO (FTCH)	Sire TAYBURN FLEET	Sire LAMMERLAW MUFFIN	Sire CONCRAIG TEAL
				Dam EIDER DELPHORRIE
			Dam TAYBURN COCKLE (FTCH)	Sire CARSWELL ZERO (FTCH)
				Dam TAYBURN RUN
		Dam GWIBERNANT SLY	Sire JASPER OF GWIBERNANT	Sire WILFRED OF HURRYON
				Dam SKEETOF HARROCK
			Dam IMP OF GWIBERNANT	Sire TEMPLEBAR BLACKIE (FTCH)
				Dam SPECKLE OF ARDOON
	Dam WINTON FOWL DOTTEREL (FTCH)	Sire CRAIG FELIN ANGUS (FTCH)	Sire WINDMILLWOOD SOCKS	Sire BUNTER OF JORDIELAND
				Dam SOOTY OF WINDMILL WOOD
			Dam NANCARROW GYPSY	Sire BUNRNTHATCH BRIG
				Dam MORBORNE TEL
		Dam NANCARROW SAFFRON	Sire NANCARROW QUICKSILVER	Sire BURNTHATCH BRIG
				Dam GWIBERNANT EBONY OF REITH
			Dam GAUDINS PSYCHE	Sire CARSWELL ZERO (FTCH)
K.C. Reg No				Dam BUSYBEE OF GAUDINS
Dam LAIGHPARK MIST (FTCH)	Sire STOORIE OF LAIGHPARK (FTCH)	Sire BUNTER OF BRUACH	Sire JORDIELAND ROB ROY	Sire SMUT OF JORDIELAND (FTCH)
				Dam JORDILAND GLORIA
			Dam JORDIELAND PENNY	Sire SPLASH OF JORDIELAND
				Dam JORDIELAND MARY ANN
		Dam BROCKMILL MEG	Sire GAVIN OF JORDIELAND	Sire JORDIELAND DANTA
				Dam BLADNOCH HONEY
			Dam JORDIELAND HONEY	Sire JORDIELAND TIP
				Dam SHIELS MIDNIGHT TRIXIE
	Dam LAIGH PARK DAZZLE (FTCH)	Sire CORWARJACK	Sire GAVIN OF JORDIELAND	Sire JORDIELAND DANTA
				Dam BLADNOCH HONEY
			Dam LUCY FEATHERS	Sire BUNTER OF JORDIELAND
				Dam HELEN OF JORDIELAND
		Dam LAIGH PARK LUCY	Sire JORDIELAND TIP	Sire CROFTMUIR SIMON
				Dam JORDIELAND TWIGGY
			Dam LAIGH PARK REITH	Sire LAIGH PARK DUFFY
K.C. Reg No				Dam LAIGH PARK BEAULAH

FIVE GENERATION PEDIGREE

Breed	COCKER SPANIEL	Breeder	Date of Birth
Name of Dog	FTCH MAESYDDERWEN KESTREL		Date of Registration
Pet Name			KC Registration No
Colour	CHOCOLATE	Owner	
Sex	DOG	MR H MILLINGTON	

PARENTS	GRAND-PARENTS	GREAT-GRAND-PARENTS	GT-GREAT-GRAND-PARENTS	GT-GT-GREAT-GRAND-PARENTS
Sire SWALLOW LAW SNIPE (FTCH)	*Sire* SMUT OF JORDIELAND (FTCH)	*Sire* GWIBERNANT EEL (FTCH)	*Sire* GWIBERNANT CAPCAJOU	*Sire* TEMPLEBAR BLACKIE (FTCH)
				Dam SPECKLE OF ARDOON
			Dam MONNOW ELIZABETH	*Sire* PINEHAWK ROBB (FTCH)
				Dam HEADLAND HAZEL OF MONNOW
		Dam DACRE JET	*Sire* JORDIELAND TIP	*Sire* CROFTMUIR SIMON
				Dam JORDIELAND TWIGGY
			Dam LUCY FEATHER	*Sire* BUNTER OF JORDIELAND
				Dam HELEN OF JORDIELAND
	Dam MISTY LAW KATY	*Sire* MIGDALE BEN OF WEAVERDALE (FTCH)	*Sire* BUNTER OF JORDIELAND (FTCH)	*Sire* CARSWELL ZERO(FTCH)
				Dam DAVINIAG OF DUCHRAE
			Dam MIGDALE LIZ	*Sire* JASPER OF GWIBERNANT
				Dam GINGER OF GWIBERNANT
		Dam MEG OF THE MILL	*Sire* RHU OF MIGDALE (FTCH)	*Sire* SOUTHFIELD SAM
				Dam GINGER OF GWIBERNANT
			Dam MERRYMAID OF BROXTON	*Sire* CARN GALVA OF BOSISTOW
				Dam LISA OF BOSISTOW
Dam WERNFFFFRWD MELYGOCH (FTCH)	*Sire* RHU OF MIGDALE (FTCH)	*Sire* SOUTHFIELD SAM	*Sire* ARDAMURCHAN MAC (FTCH)	*Sire* TEMLEBAR BLACKIE (FTCH)
				Dam TEMPLEBAR GAIL
			Dam VICTORIA OF CORSLEY	*Sire* SABLE OF CORSLEY
				Dam EXTON JULIE
		Dam GINGER OF GWIBERNANT	*Sire* ARDOON WILGO	*Sire* TIRERAGH SILVER STARLIGHT
				Dam COLLEEN OF ELAN
			Dam ARDOON ROMPER	*Sire* TEMPLEBAR BLACKIE (FTCH)
				Dam SPECKLE OF ARDOON
	Dam GWIBERNANT SNAKE (FTCH)	*Sire* JASPER OF GWIBERNANT	*Sire* WILFRED OF HARROCK	*Sire* GWIBERNANT CAPCAJOU
				Dam MONNOW MAYFLY
			Dam SKEET OF HARROCK	*Sire* TEMPLEBAR BLACKIE (FTCH)
				Dam BUMBLE OF YORKE
		Dam IMP OF GWIBERNANT	*Sire* TEMPLEBAR BLACKIE (FTCH)	*Sire* WILFRED OF CROMLIX (FTCH)
				Dam JET OF ELAN (FTCH)
			Dam SPECKLE OF ARDOON	*Sire* TIRERAGH SILVER STARLIGHT
K.C. Reg No				*Dam* COLLEEN OF ELAN

FIVE GENERATION PEDIGREE

Breed	COCKER SPANIEL	Breeder	Date of Birth
Name of Dog	FTCH WERNFFRWD ENFYS		Date of Registration
Pet Name			KC Registration No
Colour	TRI-COLOUR	Owner	
Sex	BITCH	MR H MILLINGTON	

PARENTS	GRAND-PARENTS	GREAT-GRAND-PARENTS	GT-GREAT-GRAND-PARENTS	GT-GT-GREAT-GRAND-PARENTS
Sire SWALLOW LAW SNIPE (FTCH)	*Sire* SMUT OF JORDIELAND (FTCH)	*Sire* GWIBERNANT EEL (FTCH)	*Sire* GWIBERNANT CAPCAJOU	*Sire* TEMPLEBAR BLACKIE (FTCH)
				Dam SPECKLE OF ARDOON
			Dam MONNOW ELIZABETH	*Sire* PINEHAWK ROBB (FTCH)
				Dam HEADLAND HAZEL OF MONNOW
		Dam DACRE JET	*Sire* JORDIELAND TIP	*Sire* CROFTMUIR SIMON
				Dam JORDIELAND TWIGGY
			Dam LUCY FEATHER	*Sire* BUNTER OF JORDIELAND
				Dam HELEN OF JORDIELAND
	Dam MISTY LAW KATY	*Sire* MIGDALE BEN OF WEAVERDALE (FTCH)	*Sire* BUNTER OF JORDIELAND	*Sire* CARSWELL ZERO (FTCH)
				Dam DAVINIAG OF DUCHRAE
			Dam MIGDALE LIZ	*Sire* JASPER OF GWIBERNANT
				Dam GINGER OF GWIBERNANT
		Dam MEG OF THE MILL	*Sire* RHU OF MIGDALE (FTCH)	*Sire* SOUTHFIELD SAM
				Dam GINGER OF GWIBERNANT
			Dam MERRYMAID OFBROXTON	*Sire* CARN-GALVA OF BOSISTOW
K.C. Reg No				*Dam* LISA OF BOSISTOW
Dam WERNFFRWD CI TWT (FTCH)	*Sire* RHU OF MIGDALE (FTCH)	*Sire* SOUTHFIELD SAM	*Sire* ARDAMURCHAN MAC (FTCH)	*Sire* TEMPLEBAR BLACKIE (FTCH)
				Dam TEMPLEBAR GAIL
			Dam VICTORIA OF CORSLEY	*Sire* SABLE OF CORSLEY
				Dam EXTON JULIE
		Dam GINGER OF GWIBERNANT	*Sire* ARDOON WILGO	*Sire* TIRERAGH SILVER STARLIGHT
				Dam COLLEEN OF ELAN
			Dam ARDOON ROMPER	*Sire* TEMPLEBAR BLACKIE (FTCH)
				Dam SPECKLE OF ARDOON
	Dam GWIBERNANT SNAKE (FTCH)	*Sire* JASPER OF GWIBERNANT	*Sire* WILFRED OF HURRYON	*Sire* GWIBERNANT CAPCAJOU
				Dam MONNOW MAYFLY
			Dam SKEET OF HARROCK	*Sire* TEMPLEBAR BLACKIE (FTCH)
				Dam BUMBLE OF YORKE
		Dam IMP OF GWIBERNANT	*Sire* TEMPLEBAR BLACKIE (FTCH)	*Sire* WILFRED OF CROMLIX (FTCH)
				Dam JET OF ELAN (FTCH)
			Dam SPECKLE OF ARDOON	*Sire* TIRERAGH SILVER STARLIGHT
K.C. Reg No				*Dam* COLLEEN OF ELAN

FIVE GENERATION PEDIGREE

Breed	COCKER SPANIEL	Breeder	
Name of Dog	FTCH HEATHFIELD LAD	Date of Birth	
Pet Name		Date of Registration	
Colour	BLACK	KC Registration No	
Sex	DOG	Owner	MR H MILLINGTON

PARENTS	GRAND-PARENTS	GREAT-GRAND-PARENTS	GT-GREAT-GRAND-PARENTS	GT-GT-GREAT-GRAND-PARENTS
Sire PICKLEWOOD OAK	*Sire* BUNTER OF JORDIELAND	*Sire* CARSWELL ZERO (FTCH)	*Sire* DANNY OF NORTH STANDEN	*Sire* JIMMY OF ELAN (FTCH)
				Dam DAINTY OF LADBROKE
			Dam WHISPER OF CORSEWALL (FTCH)	*Sire* GALBRY JORDIELAND PODGE
				Dam GALBRY MONA
		Dam DAVINIAG OF DUCHRAE	*Sire* WILFRED OF CROMLIX (FTCH)	*Sire* MERLIN MICKEY
				Dam NIX OF CROMLIX
			Dam TAYBURN BORGIE	*Sire* SWIFT OF ELAN
				Dam TAYBURN RHUM
	Dam SOOTY OF WIND MILLWOOD	*Sire* JASPER OF GWIBERNANT	*Sire* WILFRED OF HURRYON	*Sire* GWIBERNANT CAPCAJOU
				Dam MONNOW MAYFLY
			Dam SKEET OF HARROCK	*Sire* TEMPLEBAR BLACKIE (FTCH)
				Dam BUMBLE OF YORKE
		Dam IMP OF GWIBERNANT	*Sire* TEMPLEBAR BLACKIE(FTCH)	*Sire* WILFRED OF COMLIX (FTCH)
				Dam JET OF ELAN (FTCH)
			Dam SPECKLE OF ARDOON	*Sire* TIRERAGH SILVER STARLIGHT
K.C. Reg No				*Dam* COLLEEN OF ELAN
Dam SPEY OF SPINNINGLOCH	*Sire* CARSWELL JEREMY	*Sire* JIMMY OF ELAN (FTCH)	*Sire* SWIFT OF ELAN	*Sire* SIMON OF ELAN
				Dam BETA OF ELAN
			Dam JET OF ELAN (FTCH)	*Sire* BROOKVILLE SANDY
				Dam GEM OF ELAN
		Dam WHISPER OF CORSEWALL (FTCH)	*Sire* GALBRY JORDIELAND PODGE	*Sire* MERLIN MICKEY
				Dam JORDIELAND BUNTY
			Dam GALBRY MONA	*Sire* GALBRY DANNY BOY
				Dam GALBRY BLONDEYE
	Dam MORBORNE TEL	*Sire* HAPERSBROOK SOBERS	*Sire* EXTON MONTY	*Sire* EXTON DAVID
				Dam EXTON MOUSIE
			Dam EXTON FIZZ	*Sire* BOUY OF ELAN (FTCH)
				Dam EXTON FRECKLES
		Dam MORBORNE SPEY	*Sire* HEADLAND MUTCHKIN	*Sire* SWIFT OF ELAN
				Dam HEADLAND GINGER QUILL
			Dam MORBORNE JOY	*Sire* GREATFIELD DARKIE (FTCH)
K.C. Reg No				*Dam* EXTON FROLIC

FIVE GENERATION PEDIGREE

Breed	COCKER SPANIEL	Breeder	Date of Birth
Name of Dog	FTCH LOCH CARA BROWNIE		Date of Registration
Pet Name			KC Registration No
Colour	CHOCOLATE	Owner	
Sex	BITCH	MR H MILLINGTON	

PARENTS	GRAND-PARENTS	GREAT-GRAND-PARENTS	GT-GREAT-GRAND-PARENTS	GT-GT-GREAT-GRAND-PARENTS
Sire SWALLOW LAW TEAL	*Sire* SMUT OF JORDIELAND (FTCH)	*Sire* GWIBERNANT EEL (FTCH)	*Sire* GWIBERNANT CAPAJOU	*Sire* TEMPLEBAR BLACKIE (FTCH)
				Dam SPECKLE OF ARDOON
			Dam MONNOW ELIZABETH	*Sire* PINEHAWK REBA
				Dam HEADLAND HAZEL OF MONNOW
		Dam DACRE JET	*Sire* JORDILAND TIP	*Sire* CROFTMUIR SIMON
				Dam JORDIELAND TWIGY
			Dam LUCY FEATHERS	*Sire* BUNTER OF JORDIELAND
				Dam HELEN OF JORDIELAND
	Dam MISTY LAW SUZIE	*Sire* BLACKIE OF JORDIELAND	*Sire* CARSWELL ZERO (FTCH)	*Sire* D OF NORTH STANDEN
				Dam WHISPER OF CORSEWALL (FTCH)
			Dam DAVINAG OF DUCHRAE	*Sire* WILFRED OF CROMLIX (FTCH)
				Dam TAYBURN BORGIE
		Dam GEAN OF BEIDLIESTON	*Sire* BEIDLIESTON SPAR	*Sire* ARDNAMURCHAN MAC (FTCH)
				Dam CARSWELL WANDA
K.C. Reg No			*Dam* GENIE OF GOLDSPAN	*Sire* GOLDSPAN JET ADURE
				Dam DEBDENHALL TEAL
Dam SARA OF NOSEYWELL	*Sire* TOBIAS OF CRAIGMILL	*Sire* EXTON DANNY	*Sire* EXTON MONTY	*Sire* EXTON DAVID
				Dam EXTON MOUSIE
			Dam DELLA OF TRUNDLES	*Sire* GREATFORD BOUY
				Dam GALBRY MAGPIE
		Dam RHYND FUDGE	*Sire* BROOM OF RHYND	*Sire* PORT OF RHYND
				Dam BREACONHILL BESOMGIRL
			Dam MAY OF RHYND	*Sire* PODDLE CRAVENER
				Dam SOX OF RHYND
	Dam BRACO KIPPER	*Sire* CARSWELL ZERO (FTCH)	*Sire* D OF NORTH STANDEN	*Sire* JIMMY OF ELAN (FTCH)
				Dam DAINTY OF LADBRURE
			Dam WHISPER OF CORSEWALL (FTCH)	*Sire* GALBRY JORDIELAND PODGE
				Dam GALBRY MONA
		Dam TAYBURN RON	*Sire* WILFRED OF CROMLIX (FTCH)	*Sire* MERLIN MICKEY
				Dam NIX OF CROMLIX
			Dam TAYBURN BORGIE	*Sire* SWIFT OF ELAN
K.C. Reg No				*Dam* TAYBURN RHUM

FIVE GENERATION PEDIGREE

Breed	COCKER SPANIEL	Breeder	Date of Birth
Name of Dog	FTCH MIGDALE BEN OF WEAVERDALE		Date of Registration
Pet Name			KC Registration No
Colour	BLACK & WHITE	Owner MR H MILLINGTON	
Sex	DOG		

PARENTS	GRAND-PARENTS	GREAT-GRAND-PARENTS	GT-GREAT-GRAND-PARENTS	GT-GT-GREAT-GRAND-PARENTS
Sire BUNTER OF JORDIELAND (FTCH)	*Sire* CARSWELL ZERO (FTCH)	*Sire* DANNY OF NORTH STANDEN	*Sire* JIMMY OF ELAN (FTCH)	*Sire* SWIFT OF ELAN
				Dam JET OF ELAN (FTCH)
			Dam DAINTY OF LADBROKE	*Sire* COCOA OF POUGHLEY WOOD
				Dam DINAH OF POUGHLEY WOOD
		Dam WHISPER OF CORSEWALL (FTCH)	*Sire* GALBRY JORDIELAND PODGE	*Sire* MERLIN MICKY
				Dam JORDIELAND BUNTY
			Dam GALBRY MONA	*Sire* GALBY DANNY BOY (FTCH)
				Dam GALBRY BLONDEYE
	Dam DAVINIAG OF DUCHRAE	*Sire* WILFRED OF CROMLIX (FTCH)	*Sire* MERLIN MICKY	*Sire* GLENEWTON JULIUS (FTCH)
				Dam MERLIN MIZ
			Dam NIX OF CROMLIX	*Sire* BUOY OF ELAN (FTCH)
				Dam FRAOCH OF CROMLIX
		Dam TAYBURN BORGIE	*Sire* SWIFT OF ELAN	*Sire* SIMON OF ELAN (FTCH)
				Dam BETA OF ELAN
			Dam TAYBURN RHUM	*Sire* MERLIN MICKY
K.C. Reg No				*Dam* BRECKONHILL BESOMGIRL
Dam MIGDALE LIZZ	*Sire* JASPER OF GWIBERNANT	*Sire* WILFRED OF HURRYON	*Sire* GWIBERNANT CAPCAJOU	*Sire* TEMPLEBAR BLACKIE (FTCH)
				Dam SPECKLE OF ARDOON
			Dam MONNOW MAYFLY	*Sire* PINEHAWK ROBB (FTCH)
				Dam HEADLAND HAZEL OF MONNOW
		Dam SKEET OF HARROCK	*Sire* TEMPLEBAR BLACKIE (FTCH)	*Sire* WILFRED OF CROMLIX (FTCH)
				Dam JET OF ELAN (FTCH)
			Dam BUMBLE OF YORKE	*Sire* HEUGH HEAD MAC
				Dam HOLLY OF YORKE
	Dam GINGER OF GWIBERNANT	*Sire* ARDOON WILGO	*Sire* TIRERAGH SILVER STARLIGHT	*Sire* SIXSHOT OTTO THE OWL
				Dam TIRERAGH HARVEST MOON
			Dam COLLEEN OF ELAN	*Sire* SWIFT OF ELAN
				Dam JET OF ELAN (FTCH)
		Dam ARDOON ROMPER	*Sire* TEMPLEBAR BLACKIE (FTCH_	*Sire* WILFRED OF CROMLIX (FTCH)
				Dam JET OF ELAN (FTCH)
			Dam SPECKLE OF ARDOON	*Sire* TIRERAGH SILVER STARLIGHT
K.C. Reg No				*Dam* COLLEN OF ELAN